1

SELF-APPOINTED
ADVENTURERS

The
SELF-APPOINTED
ADVENTURERS

*Stories of Adventure from
Around the World*

NEIL HOGAN

For my family

CONTENTS

TRAVEL ADVENTURERS

ADRENALINE ADVENTURERS

DANGEROUS ADVENTURERS

COURAGEOUS ADVENTURERS

WORK ADVENTURERS

ALTRUISTIC ADVENTURERS

HEDONISTIC ADVENTURERS

MUSIC ADVENTURERS

HIKING ADVENTURERS

ANIMAL ADVENTURERS

SPORTS ADVENTURERS

"The first half of life consists of the capacity to enjoy without the chance; the last half consists of the chance without the capacity."

Mark Twain

INTRODUCTION

In 30 years, will you be ready for a life-changing adventure? Will you cage dive with a ferocious great white shark, climb to the peak of a giant mountain, jump from a bridge more than 200 metres high, throw an out of control party or sit in the cheap seats on the Indian railway?

Chances are, probably not. In 30 years, I'll probably be asking for a cup of herbal tea and a good mattress, long since exchanged from the tequila shot and a promise of no sleep 'til dawn.

In my 20s and 30s, I had solid freedom and health, so I circumnavigated the world four times as an intrepid backpacker and wrote journals. Within the pages of these holy grails, I collected hundreds of exciting stories from the people I met. They were predominantly the life experiences and adventures of stay-at-home locals alongside travellers who'd seen and done it all.

Twenty years, six continents and 60 countries later, I realised I had a pretty good collection on my hands, so with the permission of these people, I put together this book, which is a casual collection of adventurous, inspirational and occasionally crazy stories and experiences. They're told precisely as they happened, written by my self-appointed adventurers and presented as short tales.

In this book, you'll go to a party at the Playboy Mansion, get chased by a bear in Nepal, crap your pants in India, and get locked up in an American jail. You'll gain insight into bribery, what it's like to meet your idol, cycle down the world's most dangerous road, and share your room with a most wanted criminal in Australia. I will take you to all four quarters of the world, where you'll meet highly inspiring people coming toe to toe with a few bad eggs. You won't know what's hit you by the end of it!

Dreams are things you haven't got round to doing yet, so don't let them stagnate in the graveyard of ambition. It will only leave you wondering what could have been. Remember to regret the things you did and not the things you didn't do. After all, you only get one shot at life, and we're here for a good time, not a long time. So are you ready? You are. Excellent, then let's begin.

CULTURED ADVENTURERS

Yin And Yang

Kevin Massey, Senboku-machi, Japan

THE SAYING GOES THAT FOREIGNERS who have been in Japan for a day feel they can write a book about the place, those who have been there a year a chapter, and those who have stayed a decade or more struggle to write a page. I presume to share these few lines, acknowledging the reticent wisdom of the many who know more but speak less.

I arrived in Senboku-machi, a small rice-farming town in the north of the main island of Honshu, a fresh-faced, self-appointed adventurer with a head full of images of Samurai, Sake and Shinto temples, textbook representations to me of mystery and exoticism of the Empire of the Sun. But one quickly learns that these icons are neatly packaged for the tourists. To see the real Japan, the foreigner must be patient and lucky; he must observe, study, and wait for it to show itself by accident.

Nowhere is the singular and authentic character of the Japanese better displayed than in their treatment of tea or *o-cha*. In Japan, tea is drunk as a ritual more than a refreshment. Tea is sacrosanct, a cultural and historical pillar.

It presides on casual and formal occasions alike, from chatter at a friend's house to closing a business deal. This reverence is crystallised in the Japanese tea ceremony, the *Sado* (literally 'way of the tea'). A combination of meditation, grace, and controlled dexterity, the *Sado* is an intensely spiritual ritual perfected through years of dedicated practice and predicated on the complementary elements of yin and yang. In a rustic hut in Senboku, amid a knot of pine trees, I had the privilege to experience this ritual first-hand.

Fukazawa-san, a hale man in his fifties or sixties, summons his guests to the *chasitsu* (tea room) with a gong. As the ceremony host, Fukazawa-san represents yin, his guests, including me, yang. He enters from the room's northern (yin) aperture, carrying a *chawan* (tea bowl), *chasen* (tea whisk), *chakin* (a linen tea cloth), and *chashaku* (bamboo tea scoop). He greets us as we enter from the southern (yang) doorway.

A smell of incense, midwife to the divine, hangs in the air. Fukazawa-san arranges the tea bowl with meticulous precision. The bowl represents the moon (yin) and is placed next to the *mizusashi* (water pitcher), which, being bigger, symbolises the sun (yang). He sets them just so and retires to the preparation room.

Seated in the formal *seiza* position, we guests are given a chance to clear our minds, to concentrate on the simplicity of the natural and manufactured elements around us: the charcoal fire, the indoor waterfall, the carefully arranged flowers, a neatly folded silk cloth. It is a cleansing, contemplative interval.

Returning with a spoon and a bowl for wastewater, Fukazawa-san closes the northern door behind him. He proceeds assiduously to clean the bowl, whisk and scoop with the silk cloth. This cleaning is a perfunctory task; to Fukazawa-san, it embodies concentration and meditative focus.

Fukazawa-san places the utensils on the table in precise configuration with the cleaning complete. The sounds and movements of his hands are hypnotic. After what is possibly five minutes but probably fifteen seconds, he opens an ornate tea caddy and measures out quantities of powdered green tea (*macha*) into the bowl with a bamboo scoop. He adds water with the spoon and, with a controlled, nuanced motion, meticulously stirs the mixture into a luminous froth. The sounds of pouring water and a scratching whisk provide a focus for our thoughts.

This task complete, Fukazawa-san offers the bowl to Kumagai-san, the guest of honour as a town council member. Kumagai-san receives the bowl with a bow. He turns it in his hands to simultaneously admire it and ensure the front is away from his lips. He bows to me, seated on his right hand, raises the bowl in honour of the host, and sips the green viscose liquid. He passes the bowl to me after wiping the rim with a controlled and fluid action. There is reverence here, a delicacy of movement which is contagious. I take the bowl softly, raise it similarly, investigate its asymmetric beauty, and bring it to my lips. The bowl is warm, and I feel like I hold some alchemical elixir, some eastern grail. When I drink, the taste is bitter and disappointing.

I wipe the rim of the bowl and pass it on. When all the guests have taken their tea, Fukazawa-san takes the utensils and rinses them. He offers the cleaned bowl, scoop and whisk to Kumagai-san for inspection, who in turn asks permission to pass the utensils to the others present. In turn, we all carefully scrutinise and admire the tools of this curious rite. When we have finished, Fukazawa-san collects the utensils, and we bow and exit without speaking. The ceremony is over, and the guests drift apart in the company of their own counsel.

Still meditating on the anticlimax of the acrid mixture, I begin to realise that in my linear analysis, I have missed the point. This is not the west, where preparation is the means to an end, where the bottom line is all that counts, and gratification is a litany of fleeting thrills. I remember a line from the Japanese poet Mitsuo Basho who said: "*The journey is the destination.*" More than the taste of the tea, this is the essence of the *Sado*.

Lights, Sauna, Action

Eric Thurston, Nova Scotia, Canada

LIFE IS THE MOST UNBELIEVABLE trip. Each step on each road we walk down, whether mental, physical or both, leads us to enlightened moments that grant us unique precious gifts. We receive new eyes to view the world afresh, a new heart to love it to a higher degree, and fresh legs to carry us further. But through it all, I believe there are particular instances, epiphanies even, where moments culminate in a figurative snap of the fingers, and something extraordinary and entirely profound seizes us.

Whatever the circumstances for me, these special moments always occurred suddenly and intensely, sweeping me off my feet like a tidal undertow, dragging me out to incredible depths. Your epiphany may come as you watch with glistening eyes your first child entering the world or watching the sunset from a mountain peak, thousands of feet above the Earth, as you seek comfort in your lover's arms. I have cherished every one of these moments, but I want to share one phenomenal day that came along as I was considering my next steps in life. It was a day that lit up my soul.

I spent a year living in northern Finland on an exchange programme during my twenties. It was an excellent course run by Oulu University where international students from all over the world learned about Scandinavian life. During it, we had the opportunity to participate in field trips that gave us first-hand views of the quirks of living in the Arctic Circle. During one of these remarkable expeditions, I received a life-changing lesson on the astonishing beauty of mother nature and friendship.

I woke from a nap that evening with a chill in my bones, and I wondered where I was as I experienced the curious feeling of disorientation with travel. Ah yes, the cottage, my mind recalled from the previous day's bus trip to Aakenus. It was a long journey through the blustery snowdrifts of Finland's winter, but it allowed me to practice Finnish with my friend Marion. She helped me expand my vocabulary with words like 'Telephone pole,' 'Evergreen', and 'Snow,' which were the only things we saw through our frosty window.

"Eric, come outside! We have a fire started!"

The words broke into my thoughts as I rubbed the sleep from my eyes. A few of our group had started a fire inside a nearby kota, a large tepee-like structure traditionally used by the Saami people for their nomadic lifestyle. I threw on a hoody and stumbled into the group's tent to watch the fire burn. I find it fascinating how people can become so mesmerised by flames dancing, and as we sat there absorbed by the flickering light, we swapped stories while roasting *makkara*, a Finnish sausage that we covered in hot mustard.

Light can have this effect. I can stare at a fire and be swept away by its physical beauty, luring me into comfort and contemplation. Then, as the burning leads me further into my mind, I move towards a metaphysical light that offers me a perspective of life, a light through which I can detach from myself and understand the world around me.

We'd skied vigorously that day, and as our aching bodies relaxed, we prepared for that most Finnish of experiences, the sauna. Sauna is a way of life for most Finnish people, and many apartments have them as commonly as a living room or bedroom. Our sauna was a small two-room cabin, one for undressing and the other for sweating. It was a rock sauna where the stones were heated over an oven of burning wood before we poured water over them to create intense steam. The traditional way to sauna was utterly naked and preferably with an ice-cold bucket of beer at your side. Now, this I had to experience.

The girls went first, followed by the guys. A shared sauna is most common, but being foreigners, we were still a little reserved about a few Finnish traditions! When I stepped inside, it felt like the heat was at a dangerous level as it hit my lungs immediately, and I gasped as it burned its way down. Thankfully it was only temporary, and I soon adapted to the intensity. I took my place, sat down, and said the two most critical Finnish words I'd learned so far:

"Olut, kiitos," (or "A beer, please," to you and me).

Soon I was lost in my reflections of the day. Look at how beautiful nature can be, and then look back at all of us fools running around doing unimportant things. Maybe it is all about not taking these days for granted. Perhaps it is all about looking at the world and genuinely seeing her for all she has to offer. Every day, hour, minute and second. I need to appreciate everything. Every moment, every drop of water, every smile.

A few beers in, and to seize the moment, I ran from the sauna stark naked and flew through the air like an exposed spiritual superhero. It was a beautiful feeling that I hoped I'd never forget. However, instead of landing in soft, deep snow, I belly-flopped onto a pile of solid ice! I lost my pride and gained a few bumps and scrapes, but I did have some semblance of a moment, and to this day, it remains intact (along with my manhood, thankfully).

While we sat sweating in the sauna, the sun crept slowly to its bed, so when we stepped back into the tent, it made for a cosy atmosphere around our open log fire. Wherever we came from in the world, we sat together under one roof, laughing, learning and sharing lives. After a while, we heard a few people outside shouting, "Guys, come quickly".

We dashed out to find them standing with their heads tilted towards the night sky, looking up at the most beautiful image you could ever wish to see. It was the Aurora Borealis, more commonly known as the Northern Lights.

A silky white stream of light played lovingly on a black night. It glimmered and danced, swayed and swooned. I stared speechless, trying to comprehend its delicacy and captivating movement. I could hardly believe they were real. Feelings surged as I imagined a magician casting a dazzling spell across the world, bringing hope and appreciation to all who witnessed it. Gazing up at nature's performance was like watching a miracle. My friend Sandra whispered the words I would never forget.

"Now I know why God put me on this Earth."

I understood her completely. I turned my gaze slowly to my international friends, all coming together, admiring life and filled with a spark that would ultimately change us. As I stood staring into the dancing light of the Aurora Borealis, I had an epiphany. It gave me new eyes to see the world, a new heart to love it with, and fresh legs to make my way.

The two types of light I saw on that fantastic day brought the prospect of possibilities. Although I'd experienced introducing a new kind of light prism, I still considered my direction in life, which hadn't changed. But from what I learned and saw during that glorious moment, I believed I could do it in a new light.

A better light.

'La Garanta Del Diablo' (The Throat Of The Devil)

Charity Rattiner, New York, US

VACATION TIME IN THE US is holy, so when I flew to sunny Argentina for two weeks, I needed to be selective about the places I wanted to see. With this in mind, I had zero interest in making an overnight bus journey from Buenos Aries to some apparently 'miraculous falls' that lay on the border next to Brazil. I live in New York State, which is home (ok, shared home) to Niagara Falls, and in all my years of living there, I'd never had an inkling to see them either. So why would I travel more than a hundred times the distance to see some random falls in South America?

Suffice to say, I arrived in a country with a steady stream of people lined up to ask me, "So, have you been to see the Iguazu Falls yet?"

And when I'd shrug and reply with, "Well, the thing is… I haven't… and I don't think I'm going to," they'd look at me as though I'd just slapped their child.

"WHAAAAT? Are you crazy? You must be crazy. You have to go. Please tell me you'll go. You won't regret it."

And each time, I'd obligingly reply with, "Are they that good?" I'd be told, *"YES! They're THAT good!"*

I learned that the Iguazu Falls were a series of 275 waterfalls spread out over a 2.7-kilometre stretch, which was a darned impressive fact. Argentina's 'Iguazu Army' grew in influence over the following days. After hearing the same questions repeatedly, I finally caved, booking a bus ticket for an arduous 16-hour journey to a small, dusty town called Puerto Iguazu.

I met a small group of friendly European backpackers who instantly took me under their wing. The four guys had met a week prior in Buenos Aries, but by the way they traded insults, it sounded as though they'd been friends for years. I've found this common with travellers and always felt reassured that people could fall into such quick and easy friendships, despite the underlying reality of separation never being too far away.

After arriving in Iguazu at midnight, we booked into a hotel in an unkempt fashion and awoke the following day to apocalyptic weather. Grey clouds swirled the skies while torrential rain hammered down lashings of fire. This seemed unusual for a place where the sun usually shone gloriously. Though we tried to remain optimistic, the reality was a constant rain pounding a cold bedroom window with my frowning face pressed up against it. The boys donned their heavy rain gear, and, unprepared as always, I crossed my fingers and pulled out the same clothes as I would have for a sunny day.

We took a taxi to the national park, and in that short space of time, the rain stopped, moving me to punch the air with an involuntary whoop while the guys laughed and packed away their rain gear. Despite this miraculous parting of the clouds, literally hundreds of the visitors entering the park were purchasing shockingly unfashionable white plastic parkas. I strode in confidently, convinced that I'd be okay and would look better for the memorable photograph without a garbage bag. Twenty minutes later, I couldn't have been more wrong as my luck ran away with the sun. The apocalypse returned, only this time worse, and within five minutes, my jeans had doubled in weight!

As we walked the postcard-like hill paths, I seriously debated whether I wanted to be there. With each passing step, I became more of a human sponge, and even my fingers turned into prunes. I was cursing both a terrible decision of not buying a garbage bag and also the 'Iguazu Army' for convincing me to make the arduous pilgrimage in the first place. As I squelched along, with the demeanour of an utterly miserable child, we stopped at a viewing spot and were so close to a waterfall that when the spray combined with the rain, I may as well have been standing underneath the darned thing. I was utterly drenched—a little drowned rat who felt very sorry for herself.

And it was at that exact point that I let go.

I went from being an innocent party caught in a storm to admitting that I was a guilty party who hadn't prepared. And it was incredibly liberating. I no longer felt uptight or the need to control the weather. I was wet and couldn't get any wetter. And it was at that moment that the falls soaked themselves into my heart forever. Oh, if only I could begin to explain my first views of the magnificent falls after this moment. It was like walking through a mythical garden that you thought only existed in a holy book or had been destroyed by war thousands of years ago. I was awestruck.

A couple of hours in (and by that time happily squishing along at twice my normal body weight), we headed off in search of the miraculous part of the falls, heralded as its most redeeming feature: '*La Garanta del Diablo*' or '*The Throat of the Devil.*'

On your way to the *Throat of the Devil*, you have to cross a hovering catwalk perched atop the enormous Iguazu River. You begin to hear a massive roar, yet you can't quite see what's up ahead. Like a train that's thundering towards you or an orchestral crescendo that's gradually building, the roar gets louder and louder with each passing step. Then, as you walk out onto the viewing platform of *The Throat of the Devil*, it's impossible not to feel that you're just a tiny ant in its remarkable presence.

The size of the Earth is insignificant to the size of the universe. As I walked out, that was precisely how I felt. I was a being so minuscule that it felt as though I didn't exist for a brief moment. And as I stood there with the boys, the sun made its second glorious appearance of the day with the clouds parting in a kind of epiphanic moment. I tried to say something, anything, but couldn't speak properly. The sun glinted off the falling water and created a mini rainbow to feed our already overloaded senses.

The boys and I edged closer to one another and, without saying anything, looked out over the edge. The power overwhelmed us as we watched hundreds, possibly thousands of tons of water rushing endlessly over the edge with each passing second. Wave after wave of warm water soaked us repeatedly, carried by the wind and the falls themselves.

For a moment, I thought I was the only one grinning; then, I looked at the four lovely boys who'd taken me under their wing, and each of them was beaming as though we were all feeling something unique. We were blown away, caught up in a moment, excited and drenched and happy, and, oh, well, as you can probably tell, it was one of the most inspiring moments of my life.

Before you expire, you must get yourself to the Iguazu Falls in South America. I saw it once, and it completely changed my view of waterfalls forever.

The Mysterious Sea Of Ring Sting

Ian White, Leicester, UK

IN THE EARLY 1990s, I left the UK to work on a kibbutz in Israel. I was only 18, and where most of my friends were going off to party in Ibiza, I wanted to stay abroad for more than two weeks, so I had to find a place where I could combine work with partying.

I flew into a roasting Tel Aviv and went straight from the airport to an administration office for overseas volunteers. They assigned me to kibbutz Ein Gedi, located in the Judean desert on the shores of the Dead Sea and one of the better places to be placed.

After experiencing the hubbub of the city, I went to check into a recommended hostel, and even though they had no room left, they still let me check in. "No room, no problem," they said, "You can sleep on the roof!" There were over 20 of us sleeping up there that night, and when I experienced the flashes and explosions of bombs going off in the distance, I questioned whether I'd done the right thing in choosing Israel over Ibiza. The following day I was still pretty shaken as I boarded my bus to the kibbutz.

Ein Gedi is an oasis on the western shores of the Dead Sea and counts amongst its facilities a nature reserve, a guesthouse and a spa. The kibbutz is on a cliff overlooking the sea itself, which at 400 metres below sea level is the lowest point in the world. It looked like a splash of green life in an otherwise barren land from the air, and I would be spending my whole summer there. And what would be my summer job in paradise? Washing dishes!

The Ein Gedi Spa is a natural phenomenon. As well as having the Dead Sea close by, it also has thermo-mineral springs unique to Israel, bringing natural healing properties to the body. When combining this with the black mud of the Dead Sea, my skin and hair became softer than they'd ever been before. People travelled from all over the world to pay handsomely for Ein Gedi's facilities, but it was all available for free for the lucky volunteers.

Whenever I wasn't washing dishes, I'd be wallowing like a lazy hippo in my free mud bath. I'd smear large handfuls of black sludge all over my body until only the whites of my eyes showed, while my creative side conjured mohawks with colossal shoulder pads using generous amounts layered on.

To get the best results, I'd let the mud dry completely, to the point where it felt like it was a part of me. Then, as it cracked, I felt like I was falling apart like I'd been frozen and then shot with a bullet. There were showers available to rinse off, but the most satisfying method was to walk down to the Dead Sea and rinse off there. Saying this, I've since read that the Dead Sea has receded from Ein Gedi's spa, so trams now ferry people back and forth from its shores.

The Dead Sea has a salt concentration roughly ten times greater than most of the world's bodies of water, and this causes its famous floating effect that attracts people from all around the world. It has no waves, nor does it host any living fish or seaweed due to its salt levels, giving it a strange sense of eeriness. The world's only other bodies of water with higher salinity are in Antarctica, though they're probably not great for sunbathing after a swim!

Once the Dead Sea came up past my waist, I found walking difficult. My foot came up quickly enough, but I had to force it down again. A little further in, I discovered that my standing foot began to rise before I could replant my walking foot. The effect got stronger the deeper I went, and then suddenly, I was experiencing weightlessness and almost walking on water, or as close to it as I'll ever get.

If I stood up straight and leant forward, my legs involuntarily rose from behind and vice versa from the front. My naturally lazy stance was to lay back and casually sweep myself along with both arms, like a reclining water chair.

I have a warning for you, though - all good things come with a downside. Firstly, I was advised not to go anywhere near the water after having a wet shave. Normal seawater stings without compassion, but the effect of the Dead Sea on open pores was agonising. I wasn't told (and later found out to my detriment) what happens when you fart in the water. Imagine going to the toilet after a double strength vindaloo curry, and you start to come close to the ring sting I suffered. Still, that was nothing compared to the look of wincing pain on my friend's face when he tried to take a pee. It was better than any swimming pool dye, let me tell you!

Honestly, my summer days spent on kibbutz Ein Gedi were some of my happiest days. I met so many kind people and had beautiful experiences like floating in the Dead Sea that I shall never forget. My skin and hair were softer and healthier than they probably ever will be again. I have no hesitation in recommending it, and I've made a secret pact to go back there once more before I die.

Hopefully, next time I won't have to wash the dishes!

TRANSPORT ADVENTURERS

Next Stop, Novosibirsk
Donnchadha Quilty, Dublin, Ireland

I GAVE MY MUM A Post-it note before I left that summer, and upon it was a list of places I hoped to visit. She stuck it inside her kitchen cupboard, next to last year's calendar and a few taxi phone cards. There it would offer her faint hope that I knew what I was doing and could be found somewhere in Siberia if needed (they were pre-Internet days). It stayed there until I arrived back in Ireland three months later.

Carrying a rucksack of essentials, I walked out of the front door and headed for the Far East with my ever-faithful camera around my neck. All I had was a return ticket from Hong Kong and a determination to get there solely by bus and train from Russia's St. Petersburg.

I befriended Tom Dawson in a Russian hotel, whose name depicted a character from a Dickens novel. He'd embarked on his extraordinary world journey some months prior, and by a unique stroke of luck, we were taking an identical route across Russia, so we joined forces. Tom was a remarkable individual by all accounts. He had a natural zest for life and an insatiable hunger for exploration. He was also built like a brick wall and knew how to handle himself (and others) in a fight! He had tattoos and piercings and carried a hunting knife in a pouch behind his neck, like Crocodile Dundee. On the other hand, I was fresh out of university where I'd been studying science and was more likely to bamboozle a foe with a good statistic.

A few days later, we boarded a Trans-Siberian train chugging east over the vast wilderness of Siberia. "This is it", we gushed, recognising a kindred spirit in each other. "This is what travel's really about." The sun sank as a fog formed over the land, and we passed clusters of rustic wooden houses hiding in the trees, a myriad of inspiration for Russian storytellers and the first page of our bedtime tale. The Trans-Siberian railway was constructed at the end of the 19th century and is the longest railway globally at more than 9,000 kilometres. If that's not impressive enough for you, the tracks also run across *seven* time zones. How about that for a statistic?

Passengers were settling in for the night, but before we followed suit, it was time for our first Baltika beer (of many) in the dining carriage. Over the next few hours, rail workers attached a second engine to the train to haul the long line of carriages over the foothills of the Ural Mountains, a range that separates Europe from the might of Asia. It would take three nights to reach my first destination, Novosibirsk – the third-largest city in Russia – and I would become well acquainted with the dining carriage before then.

I shared my second-class sleeper compartment with three Russian women, and even though they couldn't speak a word of English, nor I Russian, we got on fine. I learned that they were staying on board until Vladivostok - the very end of the line – and I was glad we only had to share for a few days. During the day, we shuffled past each other politely, and at night I slept on a top bunk next to a window, which we kept ajar. When it proved too difficult to wash my clothes in the lavatory sink, the window came in handy for airing them. I tied a compact clothesline between two metal fixtures and was able to keep my status as a hygienic roommate by hanging my musty clothes from it. The Russian women marvelled at my apparent ingenuity.

As for washing, I tried it once in the lavatory and regretted it immediately. Apart from attempting to avoid the suspect puddles on the floor, I had to convince the aggravated person outside that I'd only be a minute, even though I was still half-naked and there wasn't enough water to rinse off the lathered soap. After that, I opted to use moist towelettes for an all-over body wash instead.

At least eating was more straightforward. Tom and I made the most of the basic food supplies we'd bought in Moscow, and our menu seldom changed. We'd mix a generous helping of canned tuna with mayonnaise and cheap black olives and then spread the mix onto dry crackers. For lunch and dinner, this was fine, but eating it for breakfast made me crave eggs like never before! Sometimes we bought fresh bread from entrepreneurial locals who'd gathered to sell food at the smaller stations, and along with tea and biscuits, this made for a welcome afternoon treat.

"I hope they're not getting onto our train," Tom had said as 100 soldiers filed past us back in Yaroslavsky Station, Moscow. "Soldiers like to do two things in their spare time – drink and fight! If they do get on, let's stay well out of their way," he advised. Needless to say, there were 100 soldiers somewhere on our train.

During the second evening, one of those soldiers strayed into our dining carriage and staggered drunkenly toward us, stepping on my foot when he got close enough. Though his stench of alcohol and sweat engulfed our personal space, we smiled and nodded, listening to him speak in Russian and returning with words like 'Irlandški' and 'Angleški,' meaning

'Irish' and 'English'. Tom kept his hand over his mouth as he spoke, which I couldn't figure out because it made him difficult to understand.

After a few minutes, the soldier left us, seemingly satisfied but more likely distracted. He reappeared a half-hour later with a badly cut face and his white t-shirt soaked in blood! He'd found somebody else to annoy during that brief interval and got into a fight. I was shocked to see the soldier bloody and bruised, but Tom wasn't surprised. "I knew something was wrong," he said. "That's why I covered my mouth - I thought he was gonna hit me." Even if the soldier had picked a fight with us, I'm sure Tom would have levelled him, only there were 99 other soldiers after him.

It took three hours to purchase our tickets in Moscow initially. Why I still don't know. A few ticket clerks refused to serve us, others came up with excessive prices and one even pointed towards the exit, telling us to leave the building altogether. It left my impression of Moscow somewhat tainted, especially when I coupled it with being kicked out of a museum in The Kremlin. I'd done little more than sit on a windowsill and make eye contact with a guard, but I still hear his whistleblowing as if I was an undercover thief about to take off with a curtain. Reading in my guidebook that the people of Novosibirsk were much less friendly than their compatriots in Moscow, I was a tad apprehensive as the train eventually pulled into the station.

Before disembarking, I blessed myself in front of the three Russian women, which I guess was a sign of my nervousness at meeting the locals. As they sat unmoved, I realised they had no idea what I was doing, so I chuckled at myself and then Tom laughed riotously at me, which they did find amusing. From here, Tom would continue to Irkutsk, and I'd join him there in a few days. In the meantime, I wished him the best of luck sharing the train with 100 crazy soldiers, knowing it was inevitable he'd have a story for me when we met up again.

I made sure I bought my onward ticket before leaving the station and surprisingly had no trouble this time. Then I strolled into the city centre and found a reasonably priced hotel where the staff members were amiable and helpful. Everything was going my way, and contrary to the guidebook's warning, everyone I came into contact with was pleasant.

The hotel lobby was a hive of activity with a busload of Americans having just arrived. I was eager to mingle with English speakers, and after introducing myself, they wanted to know why I was in Siberia looking dishevelled. After explaining my trip, they told me they'd come to Novosibirsk to adopt disadvantaged Russian children. At the same time, their interpreter added that I should visit the local Opera and Ballet Theatre, the largest in the whole country. Luckily, an Italian group was in town performing La Traviata that very night, so up in the hotel room, I had my first proper wash in days and scrubbed my clothes in the washbasin. I sang with gusto as I spruced for a grand evening ahead.

Smelling the freshest I'd been able to since leaving Ireland, I arrived at the theatre early and secured one of the best seats in the house for $20 US. I thought I'd been rather shrewd until I spoke to an astute English chap who instead bought the cheapest ticket and then sat in the 'expensive' seat next to me (a trick he'd learned from the locals).

The theatre's magnificent hall was a welcome relief from the small confines of the train's narrow carriages, and its décor was majestic, so ornate in fact that I felt transported back a century or more. The acoustics were also phenomenal, though sadly unable to keep me awake. Having so much fun had taken its toll on me, and I dropped off merely feet from the orchestra at some point during Act II. I only woke at the end when

Violetta died, joining in the rapturous applause as though I'd been as attentive as a guard dog throughout. After the show, I treated myself to a hearty meal and a pint at an Irish pub. Even in the middle of Siberia, my compatriots had surfaced to open a bar. I was so proud.

My departure from Novosibirsk was late the next night. I made it to the train on time, but when I offered my ticket and passport to the conductor, she looked at me quizzically and shook her head. She shuffled away with the documents, and I followed, hoping we could resolve the problem, whatever it was. As the minutes filtered away and the train filled, a second conductor explained that the identification number on my ticket did not match my passport number. My name alone wasn't enough, and the train wouldn't wait for me, so I made a mad dash for a ticket booth in the cavernous hall, skipped the long line and demanded my ticket reprinted. What happened next was a minor victory for the traveller away from home, as the Russian clerk obliged, albeit grudgingly in front of the outraged onlookers. A grin broke across my red, gasping face as I raced back to the platform, and the conductor punched my ticket with a minute to spare.

That night I shared my compartment with two lively Russians who attempted conversation tirelessly and guzzled Baltika beer throughout. Their hospitality meant that they wouldn't even let me buy one round of drinks. The younger chap was only a few years older than me and certainly the more animated of the two, especially when English failed him. We mimed or drew pictures expressing our thoughts (our conversation becoming a cross between Pictionary and charades). More than once, the older man encouraged me to listen to the train quietly as he grinned silently and nodded. It came to light that they repaired railway tracks in the region and were incredibly proud of their work, especially the quality of how smooth the ride was.

I opened a map of Asia and traced the path I intended to take with my finger. They could hardly believe I was planning to traverse so much of their homeland and had to call their friends to tell them! The younger one pulled out a mobile phone, dialled, spoke, and then handed it over to me. The person on the other end of the line spoke excellent English and was equally entertaining. As the phone made its way around various speakers, I suspected I'd become the topic of conversation at some party in Novosibirsk. Now I was getting the chance to tap into the real Russia, and their genuine interest in a foreigner was refreshing, even if Baltika was fuelling it!

Shortly after dawn, the two men prepared to leave the train and wrote a Russian message in my journal while I wrote a farewell note in Irish on a scrap of paper. Small things like this mean little to some but the world to others; you never know. Soon after they left, I wrote a note in my journal to advise the guidebook about their inaccurate entry on the Novosibirsk people.

After going our separate ways, Tom had been forced into a vodka drinking competition by a group of rowdy soldiers on the train. When he arrived late at night in Irkutsk, he was still suffering the ill effects of this, so he found himself a quiet spot on the floor in the station, covered up with a poncho and drifted off with his hunting knife resting on his lap. Good old Tom, I was delighted to see him waiting for me when I arrived.

We took a bus due north for eight hours the next day, arriving at Lake Baikal, the most extensive and deepest freshwater lake on Earth. It warms painfully slowly, and according to one local, ice was still floating on the surface in late spring of that year. Any visiting traveller not taking a dip is considered sacrilegious despite the low temperature. So we walked around the edge and debated the best spot to wade in. After procrastinating for 90 minutes, a cliff halted our progress, so we took that as a sign. I dived in headfirst, surfacing like a whimpering child and shaking my head to why Russians enjoyed doing this during their *winter*. Despite the freezing temperature, we encouraged one another to explore a little around the cliff face.

I took my faithful camera and waded through the bitter water until I reached a small cave where Tom was already inside. I heard him yelp unexpectedly, and he beckoned for me to come quickly and take a closer look. At first, it seemed like nothing, but then the entire wall moved. Above us, in front and to our sides, the cave was writhing, crawling and twitching with innumerable insects. With claustrophobia setting in, I realised I needed to be careful as a wrong move could have easily resulted in these insects swarming the air, and they could have been disease carriers. We retreated slowly and quietly, although not before I'd snapped a few close-ups.

Back in town, we treated ourselves to a traditional Banya sauna to try and resurrect our icy bodies. Following tradition, we sat in the hot baking room for ten minutes, walked outside, poured buckets of cold water over our heads and then whacked each other's backs with the branches of a birch tree. Then we went straight back in and repeated the process. After half an hour, I felt thoroughly rejuvenated, but I still couldn't understand why they'd want to jump into that bloody lake!

Each day my exposure to Russia reinforced that it was a country of drinking, fighting, strength, pride and brutal temperatures. My time there was drawing to a close, and a few days later, the Trans-Siberian turned south at Ulan Ude towards the border with Mongolia. After eight hours of mandatory paperwork and mindless waiting, we entered a brand new world.

Tom and I had seen and done so much already, but our adventure had only just begun. In front of us were lakes and mountains that needed exploring, the Nadaam Festival and the Gobi Desert. I had plenty of time to get to Hong Kong, and my future was yet to be written. Perhaps a celebratory drink was in order? "How about fermented yak's milk?" I asked Tom. I'd just spotted a merchant selling some through the train window.

Wise Man Says, "Bring Good Book"
Andrea Marks, London, UK

IF YOU'RE A CREATURE OF comfort, there are a thousand reasons not to travel on an Indian train. For starters, plenty of passengers have habits taught at the school of scoundrels and then put into practice in the frantic hustle and bustle of the railway system. They'll throw everything imaginable into the countryside, chasing them up with mouthfuls of phlegm, hacked forcefully from the backs of their throats.

Then, when you pull up at the stations, many fragile, old, tearful, young, scarred, scared, blind, mute, diseased or limbless beggars are coming onto the train to demand rupees from you. If you're really unlucky, you might even get confronted by a eunuch, who'll gleefully leave you a life curse if you refuse to hand over the day's desired amount.

Kids crawl around on their hands and knees with monkeys on their shoulders, sweeping the floors for a few rupees a time, seemingly innocent souls punished with hell upon this Earth.

The chai (tea) man will wake you up at ungodly morning hours, telling you once more that he sells, "CHAI, CHAI, CHAI," just in case you'd forgotten.

At times the toilets look like some poor bugger with the infamous *Delhi Belly* has had a furious go at them, aiming everywhere but the can itself. As a result, pinching your nose, aiming at a hole in the floor, and steadying yourself to the train's rocking motion becomes something of an art form.

Rubbish piles up neatly in the corners of the carriages, and it's not uncommon to see cockroaches and rats having themselves a party as night falls.

Overcrowding and overbooking are rife, testing your patience on a steaming hot day when your face is tucked into a damp, smelly armpit.

Trips that look simple on a map can take twice or three times longer than you thought, while procuring a ticket in the first place draws comparisons with taking a Hindi exam after only one lesson. Of course, this is an exaggeration, but what's not is that you'll occasionally chase your tail endlessly under a sweltering sun, getting nowhere fast.

So, considering all of these unbearable things, why on God's green Earth would you want to consider travelling on the Indian railway?

Well, as an elderly Indian gentleman with an impeccable English accent once told me, "It used to be the second-highest employer of people in the whole world." He told me this as we chugged through the countryside one afternoon in a second-class sleeper carriage, adding, "It's second only to the Chinese army." If that wasn't the fact of the century, then strip me naked and leave me out on the hill for a night.

Viewing India by train is a fascinating experience, and it goes neither too slowly nor quickly and gives you just enough time to catch the look in a person's eye as you wave to them while passing their home, field of work, or taking their morning outdoor poo.

Tea breaks become synonymous with lengthy journeys, and at three or five rupees a cup, one can get through quite a bit of 'CHAI'. Sure enough, you may feel your teeth will fall out due to the 500 or so sugars in each cup, but as an energy boost, it works like no other and breaks up your trip quite perfectly.

Spending upwards of 10 or 20 hours on a train gives you so much free time that you can start making a dent on your lengthy reading list. Over three 20-hour train rides, I managed 900 pages of War and Peace (1,400-pages in total). Whenever I think of it, this book is now synonymous with the Indian railway.

As I passed through India's immense abject poverty, I understood how good we have it in the western world, yet still we find the time to moan and bicker, talking all too often about the things we don't have rather than being grateful for what we do have. Observing from the train, I found the polarisation of India to be like no place I'd seen before or since.

Railway characters come and go in their droves. They'll be delightful, annoying, loud, obnoxious, curious, arrogant, needy, generous and downright dodgy, but rarely are they dull. As the old saying goes, 'everyone has a story to tell,' and sometimes the cliché is so apt that you don't need to try and search for another description. Most people I met treated life as a privilege rather than a right, and I liked that.

Some will want to learn English and others will want to practise theirs. One guy will ask for your opinions on his country, and then his friend will offer his own opinion on yours. Some will tell you their story, whereas the intrigued will want to listen to yours. The problematic parts of the Indian railway become accustomed to you. The wondrous parts engrain themselves in your soul.

Indian Sleeping Tablet

Laine Hong, Ohio, USA

WHEN CATCHING A TRAIN IN India, working out which carriage you're on is a self-contained mission. As the train approaches, the air hangs heavy with humidity and sewage, and the platforms come alive in a writhing mass of people, so manoeuvring with a backpack is an arduous affair for anyone.

The train system has first, second and third-class carriages, and I made it a rule to mostly budget travel in second-class, aside from the one time I picked up a bargain on the price of a third-class ticket. The journey in question lasted seven hours, and the cost of my ticket was 47 rupees - the equivalent of less than $1 in 2005. A seven-hour train journey in the US would have set me back 50 times the price.

In another moment of madness, I once took a 20-hour bus journey from Hampi to Mumbai and followed it straight up with a 20-hour train ride to Rajasthan two hours later. The bus trip went off without incident, but I'd have to say that my night on the train was the most challenging and bizarre public transport experience to date.

Sleeping tablets are easy to obtain in India, and the only time I ever encountered a problem, I said to the pharmacist, "You know what, you have a great country, but I'd like it even more if I could sleep properly." Being fiercely proud of his homeland, the guy wanted me to enjoy my stay and duly prescribed a batch. These tablets were most beneficial for the long and turbulent night passages through his crazy country, except during this one trip to Rajasthan.

I'd booked a second-class sleeper, and as I stood swaying in the platform's heat waiting for the train to arrive, I couldn't wait to fall back into an empty bunk. When it pulled into the station, I looked on as my porter scanned the printed list of passengers attached to the outside of each carriage, a unique approach adopted by the Indian railway system. My porter was a tall, stocky fellow who barged his way through the hordes with my backpack on his head, elbowing whoever got in his way and shouting defiantly at those who dared confront him. I tipped the guy extra and thanked my lucky stars he'd been available. I'm too polite to barge people out of the way without feeling rude, so paying this guy to do it was a guilty pleasure.

There were nine beds in the busy compartment (three triple bunks), but no one was interested in returning my smile. Holding the ticket, I pointed toward the top bunk I'd been assigned but which had already acquired ample luggage from the others. I showed the ticket to a middle-aged man sitting underneath, who nodded and said something loudly. Everyone laughed, and after putting me down, he took the bags down.

With my trusted and well-travelled fleece as a pillow, I lay on the bed, placing the backpack at my feet and pulling out my book. For the next eight hours, I pretty much kept this posture, although, at one point, I did move my backpack to lock it up underneath the bottom bunk on the filthy carriage floor.

After a late dinner of dal and rice, I squinted through a few final pages of small print and timed it precisely with taking two sleeping tablets so I'd fall asleep as the carriage lights went out. I hoped to wake up in Rajasthan 10 hours later, ready to embrace all it would inevitably throw at me. I waited 30 minutes for the tablets to kick in and then climbed down to brush my teeth, noticing how unbelievably littered with rubbish the corridor was. Five minutes later, and with my teeth clean, I lay back on the top bunk and drifted off into an instantly deep sleep.

I awoke with a startle, wholly disorientated. I looked down to see the disgruntled middle-aged man from earlier grabbing at my leg and shouting something that I didn't understand. He appeared to be telling me that I was in his bed and to get out, so I told him he was mistaken and turned my back. He persisted, only louder. I told him to go away, only louder. I was asleep within seconds, drifting off while he was still ranting.

Once more, I awoke with a startle, feeling all at sea and with my eyelids trying to weld themselves back together. Standing next to the bed was a ticket collector in uniform speaking clear English and commanding my attention. I sat up and wearily told him my version of events, almost as though I'd been deprived of sleep for days and confessed to a crime I hadn't committed.

"I am very sorry for bringing you the bad news," he said, shaking his head, "but this is not your bunk... you are the bottom bunk."

I might have taken out my ticket to challenge him if I'd been alert, but hearing that the issue could quickly be resolved was reassuring. The tablets were making decisions for me, so I clambered into the bottom bunk and dropped off again.

Not long later, I was woken again. This time it was someone tapping my leg and muttering quietly. The new guy looked like the father of the man upstairs, possibly even the grandfather. He was about 80 years old, had a short white beard, and was trying to tell me that I was now in *his* bed. I shook my head and laughed it off, feeling like Goldilocks. In a blurry haze, I ignored the old man and went back to sleep. A few minutes later, the ticket collector came back, but he had a little black book with him this time.

"I am very sorry," he said with a rhythmic shaking of the head. "I have the bad news to deliver that your bed has been double-booked."

"You what?" I said incredulously. "What do you mean you've double booked my bed? How do you even double book a bed?" Even though I managed to string these sentences together, it was a terrific struggle, due to being so dazed.

"Sometimes it happens… today it happened because it is a very busy New Year's train… many families are going back north, sir."

As he said this, he showed me his black book and pointed to two numbers that were the same, like a short administration lesson on the Indian railway ticketing system. He closed his book with a kind of 'and that's the end of today's lesson' look and a defiant nod. All I could muster in return was, "But it's January 9th, damn it… New Year was ages ago… this is darned ridiculous."

My frustrations weren't helping the old man. He'd stayed standing throughout, yet he hadn't raised his voice once or asked for help from anyone. Something in his face made me feel like I was being a right shit for refusing him somewhere to sleep. That something gave.

I made it very clear that the bed was divided down the middle.

"We are NOT sleeping top and tail," I stated while he waggled his head. "If we crouch into little balls like this [demonstration], we can both sleep here. Don't put your feet on my side, and I won't put my feet on your side. Do we have a deal?" His head was waggling enthusiastically now, an endearing Indian style that I found rather disarming.

Despite my haggard state, the ticket collector and the old man both seemed happy, so at least that was something. I was exhausted and agitated, which only got worse five minutes later when I awoke to the old guy's feet not two inches from my nose. I'm sure you don't need me to tell you that after a humid day walking around the train, his feet were far from smelling of roses!

I sat up and woke him, re-iterating that we had two sides to the bed, "One for you and one for me." He smiled and waggled his head. I again showed him what a crouched ball looked like, and he copied me, so I sat awake watching him for a couple of minutes as he needed to understand his part of the bargain. He looked like he did.

We were crossing from the country's south to the north, and I noticed the temperature outside dropping significantly. I pulled the window up as far as it would go and thought that I'd be ok if I could get some sleep.

As you might have guessed, 10 minutes later, I woke to find the little scamp's feet in my face once again. Patience is usually a strength for me, but the thin ice I was standing on fell through. I sat up, grabbed my cigarettes and walked to the end of the carriage to calm down.

As I smoked a cigarette out of a window, I realised that I hadn't planned for the cold night ahead, and it would be a long time before I saw the sun again. I walked back to my section, past the cosy passengers wrapped up in their warm blankets and who I now totally despised. I'd been so engulfed in the hot south Indian weather that I hadn't considered how different the north might be. As a result, I wore nothing more than thin combat trousers and a t-shirt. India had well and truly caught me with my pants down.

I attempted to get into my backpack underneath the bottom bunk, but it was now too far back as someone had locked their luggage in front of it. It could have been any of the other nine in my section who were all snoring like old cats, oblivious to the wretched character on hands and knees beneath them, shivering in the lessening temperatures. Sacrificing my pillow for warmth, I pulled the faithful fleece around me and sat next to granddad's feet on the bottom bunk, resting my head against the side. With the train's jerky motion, I could only sleep for a minute at a time before being jolted back to bitterly cold reality.

I don't know how long I tried this, but I eventually gave up and began wandering the train, deliriously looking for anywhere else to sleep. *Anywhere*. I walked the second-class cars to first-class, checking every bed for a spare, but all were taken. When I arrived at first class, they wouldn't let me in; besides, no beds were available, they said. I walked in the opposite direction until I got to the start of third class, some 15 or 20 carriages back, maybe more. The first one I entered was packed solid with people, and after seeing this, I realised my situation could have been far worse. I can't imagine how uncomfortable it must be to sleep in a third-class Indian carriage, even for one night.

I grabbed my smokes again and walked erratically to the carriage door window. I'd turned into a red-eyed, smiling, drooling, delirious loon on the verge of severe irrational thought. As I stood there smoking, I eyed up a collection of rubbish in the corner that began to look like an appealing mattress. Once I'd rationalised sleeping on it, a rat scuttled out, looked at me, and darted back in. Even the rodent had a bed for the night.

I looked at my watch - it was 2 am. The sun wouldn't begin to warm the carriage again until at least 6.30 am. I stumbled back to my end of the bed and sat back. When granddad manoeuvred himself, so his feet rested on my lap, I didn't bother moving them. I was shattered and broken, shivering in the cold north Indian air. Along with those blasted sleeping tablets, the Indian railway system had snapped me in two.

Tomorrow it would make for a decent story, I thought.

I couldn't wait for tomorrow to arrive.

True Romance

Glenn Rankin, New Zealand

I WILL NEVER FORGET A Bolivian night bus I once took from La Paz to Sucre, even if I wanted to. A hypnotist couldn't remove that scar from my memory. Sure, I can smile about it now, but at the time, I thought I was going to kill someone.

I was squeezed into a cramped wooden seat behind a short, stout Bolivian couple to set the scene. Predictably, the bus was delayed for an hour, so the couple used that time to get hammered drunk on a bottle of local whisky. I was quietly impressed when the wife polished off the last part with a few hefty chugs, though I knew things would be getting unpredictable from that moment onwards.

About an hour out of La Paz, the sun went down and the bus became dark. The husband then stood up, stumbled into the aisle, pulled a plastic bag out of his pocket, and shook it open, attempting to urinate into it. Due to his drunken state and the terrible potholed roads, his piss splashed all over his hands and onto the floor as he went full throttle. Despite this, he kept going until he finished, tying a knot in the bag and placing it down by his feet, not two feet from my daypack! I laughed as he wiped his wet hands on his shirt and sat back down.

Not content with one bottle of whisky, the couple produced another from their bag, and while opening it, the husband lost his grip (possibly due to the urine), dropping it onto the floor and smashing it outright. Breaking the bottle on its own wouldn't have been so bad, but he burst the bag of piss too! My daypack was instantly soaked right through in whiskey and urine. I was mighty angry at this and shouted a few choice words in Spanish, but he didn't seem fazed. Ten minutes later, he conjured another large bottle from their never-ending stash.

A few hours down the line, the bus stopped for a toilet break, and we all got off. After getting back on, I noticed as we pulled off that the wife hadn't returned (the husband had passed out immediately after emptying his bladder again). It might have been a spiteful act, but I didn't care. They hadn't apologised for soaking my bag in piss, so I said nothing.

I grinned to myself at what was about to unfold. We made 15 minutes before the husband woke up and panicked big time. He stumbled to the front to explain to the driver what had happened, and from what I could make out, the driver told him he couldn't go back. This set the guy off, and after plenty of arguing, the driver relented, turning the bus around and going back.

As we got closer, I could see her waving frantically from a distance and knew we were in for some entertainment. As we pulled up, the look on her face suggested that her husband had left her behind on purpose, and she was ready to explode. Even though we were near the back, I could hear her shouting profanities before she was even back on board. By the time she reached us, she screamed wildly and launched herself at him, punching him in the face and body as he tried to defend himself.

After lots of scratching, hair pulling, punching, slapping, and swearing, she finally settled down, only to kick off at least once every hour for another six hours for the rest of the journey. Sure, it made for decent entertainment, but I will never get the smell of that whisky urine cocktail out of my memory for as long as I live.

Princess Elbows

Angelo Nih, Queensland, Australia

TRAVELLING TEACHES YOU MANY VITAL lessons in life. Make sure your street food is steaming hot before you eat it, don't drink the tap water in developing countries, keep one eye on your bank account, and never drink copious amounts of beer before taking an overnight bus in Bolivia.

Following an afternoon of doing the latter, I climbed aboard the most decrepit, sorry-looking bus I'd ever seen and sat down in a cramped wooden seat, preparing for an expected brutal hangover over the coming hours. Actually, 'sitting' in my seat wasn't accurate; I was more crouched into a ball with my bare knees jarring against the seat in front. Bolivians aren't the tallest of people, and spacious seats on Bolivian buses were a non-entity.

I battled through 60 minutes before the headache kneed me in the groin, a despicable act that coincided with the bus stopping to pick up Bolivia's fattest woman with the world's largest elbows. As she heaved her gigantic frame onto the bus (akin to an elephant squeezing into a Mini), I realised that the only seat left was with yours truly. She surveyed the bus, and by the way she pinned me to the corner with her stare alone, she didn't look too chuffed about being my bus buddy either. Helping conceive my first ever pangs of real claustrophobia, she squashed me against the side, and I wondered who I'd been in a previous life - Al Capone, Genghis Khan, Hitler, basically anyone on the naughty list.

Our shit heap old bus had boiling pipes running its entire length by the window passenger's feet, and due to my partner's size, I had scant room for manoeuvre. To cope with the constant cramp in my buttocks, I had to try and wrestle my knees underneath the seat in front to circulate the blood. And each time I succeeded, I was rewarded with two scraped knees and a scorched left ankle!

Between my partner's gigantic left elbow sporadical-ly jabbing me in the ribs, the dreadful roads of Bolivia, the bus's lack of suspension, the pipe burns and the 100-degree bus temperature with absolutely no working windows, I was having a ball. In addition, the afternoon beers had stretched my bladder to breaking point, and if someone had offered me an adult nappy at that point, I'd have paid top peso. With no idea when we'd stop, I had to concentrate fiercely on quelling the body's repeated threat of popping its kidneys. Finally, after what felt like three days but was more likely three hours, the bus pulled over to the side of the road.

I turned to get past my Bolivian princess only to find that she was asleep and could be woken by no man. Unsure of what to do, I climbed over her mountainous body, careful not to step on any crevasses that might give way. Once over, I ran off the bus and behind a dedicated wall for the most gratifying leak of my life that lasted around five minutes, a bladder marathon in the peeing world. Whoever overheard my audible pleasure would easily have misinterpreted it as an extra-curricular activity rather than an innocent draining.

Feeling chipper, I strutted over to a vendor and bought my daily packet of biscuits (in Bolivia, I found that all villages sold either bland biscuits or what looked like boiled monsters, so I often opted for the biscuit diet or nothing at all). I began to climb over the elephant back on the bus, but she woke up and shouted accusingly. I apologised profusely and squeezed myself back into my prime real estate, proudly boasting one square foot.

For the next eight hours, I experienced a continued repeat of these frustrations and tried to soften the blow by using my partner's fleshy upper arm as a pillow. Each time she woke and noticed this, she rebuffed my approach with a firm one to the ribs. I finally dropped off at about 5 am, roughly 10 hours after first sitting down.

I woke at 6 am as we pulled into a local bus station, and the passengers disembarked, including Princess Elbows. Before our sorrowful goodbye, I asked her if we were in Potosi, and she replied that it was still an hour away. I fell asleep again instantly.

Fifteen minutes later, a crazed Bolivian man with blood-shot eyes was standing over me shouting. I was tired, confused and just wanted him to leave me alone. When I calmed him, I realised that Princess Elbows had spun me a yarn, and we were already in Potosi. I had a little chuckle.

Why had she done it, I wondered. Had she taken offence to me climbing over her? Had she heard me relieving myself after the beers? Had she wanted both seats? Well, if I'd been a lousy bus partner, then so had she.

Oh well, I thought as I peeled myself off the seat. I could feel a great weight lifting itself from my shoulders, my arse, and my whole body.

TRAVEL ADVENTURERS

A Short Honeymoon Bike Ride

Beat Zbinden, Villarrica, Chile

IT WAS REMARKABLE THAT IT took just one day for Claudia and me to make a decision that would change our lives forever. Such a small amount of time affected such a large amount of our future. We were on tour from Switzerland to Norway when we first decided to motorbike the world together.

A couple of years later, having finished our studies and saved every franc from tedious part-time jobs, we saw it as our defining moment to pull the trigger. We'd read about a Swiss couple cycling from Alaska down to Patagonia, and quite out of nowhere, this inspired us to replace our motorbikes with bicycles instead. It wasn't a decision we took lightly, though it all seemed to happen very quickly from that moment. I married my sweetheart in August, and we left in September after selling everything we owned.

We set out with no structured plans, no sponsors, and no goals. All we had left in the world was our bikes and what we carried on them. We had a couple of visas for India and lofty ambitions to make it to mysterious, shrouded Tibet, perhaps even vast Australia.

Our first weeks in Italy, Greece and Turkey were more tiring than anticipated. It took us time to build the leg muscles we'd need to spend every day on heavily loaded bicycles. But as the days passed, we grew fitter and more robust, gradually adapting to our new method of travel. We started at a slow pace and did not need to hurry.

We made it to Istanbul and then flew onto Delhi, India, which differed from extremes. Having experienced slight changes day to day in Europe, we found this change a little too severe. After our first impressions of India, we realised that travelling by bicycle had been our best decision. There were no dramatic changes in people or landscapes from one day to the next, which gave us time to acclimatise slowly. The slower the speed, the better our travel experience was.

Cycling on India's lawless roads always felt dangerous. Lorries and buses sat at the top of the Indian survival ladder while pedestrians and cyclists clung to the bottom. Despite the daily struggle for survival, our time there was remarkable. Few areas of the world have such a variety of landscapes, cultures, people, and unbelievably delicious food. We spent six months cycling around this incredible and unforgettable country.

Having survived India, we felt ready to take on anything, and the subsequent 'anything' just happened to be the gruelling Himalayas! We passed through Nepal in an attempt to enter Tibet via the Friendship Highway, and though a few backpackers told us that the border was closed to individual travellers, we decided to go and check it out for ourselves. We learned that you shouldn't always believe what other travellers tell you; sometimes, you have to go and find out the truth for yourself. When we arrived at the border, we found we could cross into shrouded Tibet without any interference from border control. For us, this was a huge dream come true.

We celebrated with a mammoth 160-kilometre climb to Lalung pass, 5050 metres high. Cycling at that altitude was taxing, but sitting at the top of a breath-taking pass (quite literally) helped take the edge off our suffering. One month and 1000 kilometres later, we finally reached the mystical city of Lhasa, the capital of Tibet.

Having been advised that all roads from Lhasa to South China were off-limits to foreigners, we planned to fly back to Nepal and then onto Thailand. However, just before buying our plane tickets, we met a couple of western cyclists who'd pedalled up to Lhasa from Kunming in the south. Maybe our next challenge was one that we hadn't even anticipated. Could it be possible to cycle 1600 kilometres, on gravel roads, across a restricted area of the Himalayas? With optimism still fresh in our hearts, we thought, why not try it at least.

We left Lhasa at the beginning of July on fully loaded bikes. There'd be no chocolate available for the entire route, so we carried 40 bars each, a reliable energy source. As it turned out, food was a significant problem on the Yunnan Highway as we couldn't find any, so the chocolate saved us on more than one occasion. On top of being constantly hungry, we endured awful roads with deep craters, wild dogs chasing us, vomit-inducing passes, corrupt police officers and plenty of storms.

Our first major challenge came on 400 kilometres when we arrived close to a checkpoint well known for its unfriendly police officers. Cycling at midnight was no fun, but we had no choice. It was either sneak by, pay a heavy fine, or worse still, risk our bikes being confiscated. Thankfully we tiptoed past them like silent assassins during the night and continued unaffected.

We came to a tricky section a week later where an enormous landslide had wiped out the entire road. It took four hours to precariously navigate the slippery boulders and get our bikes over to the other side, but again we battled through without injury.

Having survived these challenges, we got caught by police officers two days after the landslide and were convinced that our hopes would be squashed. And had it not been for the massive landslide behind us, they most certainly would have been. Even though the policemen couldn't speak English, and we couldn't speak Chinese, we could describe the situation through animated hand gestures. Our communication somehow worked, and they agreed to let us pass. We could scarcely believe our luck.

A little further down the pass, we had a near-death experience that made us wonder why the hell we'd gone so deep into the mountains. Early in the afternoon, we were travelling through a narrow valley when a thunderstorm kicked in and with it the sound of loud clicking. We stopped in our tracks as rocks passed directly over our heads and realised we were in a rockfall. I do not doubt that we'd have died if it hadn't been for a solid wall behind us, protecting us from the frighteningly large boulders. The experience left us severely shaken and wondering whether we'd make it out of the mighty Himalayas alive.

On our first wedding anniversary, we emerged from the mountains and reached Shangri-La (Zhongdian as it was then), a small city in the province of Yunnan. As a part of our celebration, we thanked the mountain gods for surviving the most challenging part of our trip. From here, travelling to Kunming was relatively easy, and once there, we cherished being in a city again after so much isolation. Food was abundant once more, teaching us never to take it for granted again, no matter our life situation.

We'd been on the road for one year and covered almost *13,000 kilometres*, a significant portion of it on some of the world's highest gravel roads. As a result, we'd changed physically and mentally as people. Time still wasn't an issue, and we had all the time in the world. We stayed at the places we liked for as long as we wanted, living frugally and deciding that we'd become our own bosses when the time was right. We also had tremendously strong bodies and could cover much larger daily distances than before.

We cycled through Thailand and sampled their many exciting dishes, the best food we'd eaten in over a year. Then we dropped into Malaysia, and from the little we saw, we thought it was stunning. If we hadn't been so excited about the thought of Australia, we'd have stayed longer, but we did promise to visit again someday.

From Penang, Northern Malaysia, we took a speedboat to Medan on the island of Sumatra, finding Indonesia to be similar to India, though less chaotic. The markets were the most colourful in Asia, and we found ourselves exploring them endlessly. For four months, we island-hopped across Indonesia, eventually reaching Timor. After more than a year in Asia, it was our time to say goodbye, so we boarded a plane to Darwin in Australia's sweltering Northern Territory.

Australia impressed us through its immense size and endless uninhabited land. It was roughly the same size as the United States mainland but with 20,000,000 people rather than 300,000,000. Coming from Switzerland, we weren't used to cycling for days without speaking to anyone, but that's precisely what we got in Oz. As we crossed Australia's baking Red Centre, we were alone again, contrasting the desert's empty silence with the thousands of people who'd stared at us in Asia. The cycling wasn't easy, especially in the heat, but the striking landscapes made for unforgettable sunsets and sunrises, and we lost count of the number of photography opportunities.

Certain aspects of a horizon can easily be missed when travelling in a car or bus. We found the perfect speed to appreciate our senses was the speed of a bicycle. Realistically, the body can adjust to pedalling 100 or more kilometres in a single day, making it possible to cover a decent amount of ground without any dramatic changes.

To help cut costs in Australia, we always stayed on campgrounds and cooked our meals. We hadn't eaten much meat in Asia, but we made amends by boiling up plenty of Aussie beef and potatoes in the evenings. We cherished sleeping out in the bush so much that we'd only slept in a bed three times by the end of our six months there.

The following country on our tour was New Zealand, where we zipped around both islands in record time. We found it a stunning and friendly place, though the roads weren't as tricky as we'd been led to believe, which was strangely disappointing. We demanded a fresh challenge involving a massive push to compensate for it.

We decided to attempt to cycle from Patagonia in the south of South America to Alaska, the very north of North America, for the ultimate adventure. It would be in the region of some *25,000 kilometres*! If we'd been in the Himalayas when we set this goal, I'd have thought the altitude was getting to us, but the mountains had helped create a passion and determination to construct enormous plans like this.

Starting from Punta Arenas, we slowly crept north through Chile and Argentina, crossing the lonely pampas on Ruta 40, followed by the wet and wild Carretera Austral. In Bariloche, we met Benjamin, a fascinating German man who had lived and worked in South America for many years. He told us of his experiences living there, and it sounded as though he had a rewarding life.

One week later, we arrived in Villarrica, a small town in the Chilean Lake District, and we never left. After 30 months and *33,000 kilometres* on the road, we stumbled upon our new home in Chile. Similarly to the decision for the world trip itself, our plan to settle was taken remarkably swiftly, almost from one day to the next. We'd fulfilled our dreams and couldn't be more grateful. We'd arrived in a place where we felt we could start the next adventure.

It's been some years now. Claudia and I have started a small family and opened a friendly backpacker hostel in Villarrica (*Torre Suiza*). Every morning I wake up and laugh to think that we cycled here from Switzerland. It was such a long way.

Travelling the world by bicycle was one of the most incredible and inspiring things I'll ever do. Of course, it wasn't a decision carried out easily, but like a rockfall, it wasn't easy to stop once it gathered momentum.

I'm happy that Claudia and I dared to follow our dreams.

From Here To Tranquillity

Neil Hogan, UK and Ireland

I COULDN'T WAIT TO GET the hell out of Cartagena, which was funny as I once couldn't wait to get there. The food was terrible, the people were intent on scamming me constantly, and the horns of taxis blasted non-stop between 8 am and 10 pm. In fact, towards the end of my time there, I got massively irate whenever I heard a taxi driver hold his horn for more than three seconds. The din would incite me to hurl a volley of abuse from my balcony towards the sea of death traps and their drivers below, even though I was unaware of the culprit. A street vendor would smile as he looked up at me; such was the normalcy within that insane bubble.

The decrepit hotel I'd booked into stood out from the first moment I saw it, and like a drunken romantic, I envisaged finishing this book within its rotting walls. However, once I became a resident there, I began to feel more like a character in a Hunter S Thompson novel, slowly going insane as a prisoner of war subjected to Chinese water torture of the ears. Still, I stuck it out for its friendly staff and the view from my balcony, albeit a highly dusty one that could miraculously transform itself within an hour of being swept. And from my dusty balcony, I watched the craziness of Colombia's Cartagena High Street unfold from a safe distance.

Before I arrived there, I'd researched my next trip to Panama, finding that overland travel was highly discouraged as rebel guerrillas kidnapping western tourists in the area was not uncommon. Adventure was high on my agenda; getting kidnapped was not. I was told that despite these dangers, a few illegally chartered boats would happily take you island hopping in the Caribbean Seas and then deliver you safely to the other side. This idea sounded too good to be true. I would see desert islands, travel to Panama, and have a boating adventure.

For the first two weeks, I didn't encounter another backpacker at my hotel, so unsurprisingly, the receptionist had no information about illegally chartered boats. As a result, I began approaching random backpacker-looking types on the street, though I struggled to get solid information and was amazed at how fast people walked off when I mentioned 'illegal'. However, one Australian chap wasn't fazed (good old Aussies), and told me that I'd find what I wanted down at the docks. 'Illegal' and 'docks' often go hand-in-hand, so it made complete sense.

The following day, sweating like a cheese sandwich in the middle of a well-attended pickle convention, I made my way down to the dodgy docks in the blazing Cartagenian heat. I'm not kidding when I say it was roasting. My back sweat was leaking through an initial t-shirt, then through the first layer of the backpack, seven more t-shirts inside, and to the other side of the pack. I was a walking, glowing, sweating pig of a man.

The only person I found at the docks that day was the shadiest looking Colombian in Cartagena. He looked like a disgruntled, retired wrestler who'd just been woken from two months of hibernation and would joyfully have pounded my head simply because he missed the warm feeling it gave him.

He grunted that it was pointless looking for a boat: "Uh… bad weather coming, hombre… no boats sail until next week."

This news was a significant body blow as I'd planned on escaping soon, and my days of horn blasts were quickly mounting up. Cartagena had become a time vampire, and I was the reluctant victim, so I clung to the romance of finishing the work I'd started, holing myself up in the hotel with its world of mayhem mere metres from the balcony. Let the storms roll in, and the honks continue.

Five days and three million honks later, I followed up a couple of backpacker leads, which led me to David, pronounced 'Daveed'. He was a skipper from France who had settled down with a Colombian lady some years prior.

"Once they get their hands on you, amigo, life is never the same," he told me with a smile and a wink.

To be fair to Daveed (I took great satisfaction in pronouncing it as though I, too, were a Frenchman), he seemed a genuinely happy soul, especially as his wife was due to have their first baby after his next Panama run. He looked slightly crazed and wouldn't take any shit from his passengers, and he also said he'd let me steer the boat, so I immediately liked him. Even though he was only thirty-two, he looked fifty-two, which added a little weather-beaten security to my doubts about his yacht navigating capabilities.

He pitched the illegal voyage to me confidently over a gritty cup of coffee, and before I knew it, I was handing over my tatty hard-earned dollars. He gave me a date and time to meet him at the Boat Club at the docks, and in return, I gave him a few hundred dollars and my passport. As with every other time I've done this, I cursed my naivety and trusted my faith in humanity. Still, I was thrilled to finally set sail, especially as I'd exceeded writing targets despite the mental honking barriers. Hunter would have been proud.

I arrived at the agreed time two days later, but there was no sign of Captain Daveed or any of his passengers. A half-hour passed, and though my concern was growing, I felt reassured that I'd been in far worse situations before and could replace a passport and some dollars. I could not say the same for my faith in humanity.

An hour later, I was laid flat out on a wooden pier staring absent-mindedly at the sky when the first two passengers, a stringy Swiss guy and his dainty Spanish girlfriend, crept into my peripheral vision. We got chatting, and from first impressions, they were a quintessentially well-rounded European couple; intelligent, bilingual, probably charitable, genuinely intrigued by the world, and your A1 types for how world leaders desire their citizens to be, especially the Swiss.

Their arrival helped alleviate any fears about Daveed having done a runner, mainly as I'd laid there dwelling on stories about the availability of dodgy passports in Colombia. I had never suspected being done over by a scrawny Frenchman, though.

A fresh collection of moody clouds decided to open for business, pounding us with the most enormous raindrops I'd ever seen. We ran for shelter inside the Boat Club. On hearing we were with Daveed, though, they told us to piss off (or Spanish equivalent). Intriguing. We took it on the chin and got soaked through, bags and all, with nowhere else to go. Things weren't going well.

Fifteen minutes later, as the rain stopped and the clouds parted, we heard a car honking its horn (!), and our scraggy skipper appeared like Moses with a staff in a taxi filled with torn hessian sacks of fresh fruit and vegetables. Daveed looked like he'd just been released from jail, and at first glance, I thought he'd also been caught in the rain, but he'd just been sweating on closer inspection. His delay and appearance made sense when he said he'd had some 'unexpected complications' at the Colombian passport office. He handed me a sack with potatoes leaking from one of its holes, and my faith in humanity lodged itself firmly back in my heart.

Daveed murmured as though he was talking to everybody and nobody simultaneously for the next ten minutes, often making non-decipherable statements and then laughing out loud. It was perfect casting if he was acting out the role of a clichéd sea captain who'd gone slightly mad after years at sea. He sure was an oddity, and I thought he was great.

The last three passengers arrived two hours late but were quickly forgiven as they had five beer boxes. The three guys represented England, Australia and Switzerland, the lands of alcoholism, rampant gambling and fresh air. I'll let you assign which was which.

Daveed planned to sail for roughly thirty-eight hours until we reached the San Blas Islands at dawn on the third day. The San Blas Islands are an archipelago of 365 islands off the east coast of Panama (one for each day of the year if you're feeling extravagant). They're situated to the east of the Panama Canal but surprisingly don't attract many tourists, though they are a hard-to-reach paradise and something of a hidden gem for those who know about them.

We slowly motored out to the gulf of the harbour and were faced with an endless carpet of soft blue waves marching into the horizon. The late chaps had started drinking heavily from the moment they arrived, so it wasn't long before seasickness set in, and they were blowing chunks over the side of the boat. Luckily I'd stayed off the brew for a few days, so my sea legs held firm, and along with our zany skipper, I devoured any food that appeared.

I was surprised that Daveed had chosen to take as many as six passengers for a small yacht, especially when we realised that there were only six beds for seven people. Rather than start a mutiny on our first night, though, we laughed at his entrepreneurial skills and vowed to make do. It was an illegally chartered boat, after all.

Daveed's food wasn't exactly what you'd get in a French restaurant or café, but he did cook three meals a day for five days in a swaying kitchen, so I take my apron off to the guy. When I did the math, it came to over a hundred meals, which was a solid effort for a guy who initially looked like he'd struggle to boil water.

"Geezer, come up on deck and check this out," said Phil the Englishman as I woke groggily on the third day. During the night, I'd taken watch of the yacht as we sailed through without stopping, finishing my shift at 4 am. I heaved myself up the steps to a sight that most people only dream about on their work screensavers over morning coffee. We'd finally reached our destination.

A picture-postcard desert island lay ahead with golden sand, lush green palm trees, and small lapping waves making identical slaps. The water was so clear you could see the ocean floor at ten metres, and we were the only tourists within miles. Upon dropping anchor, our barmy skipper's first action was to strip down to a pair of dirty y-fronts and dive straight in. Quicker than you could say, "Wash those underpants, you dirty Frenchman," I too was diving off the back of the boat into the most transparent water I'd ever experienced. I will never forget that first dive for as long as I live.

I swam fifty metres to the island and dragged myself onto the sands like the survivor of a shipwreck. It was just past 6 am, and the sun was appearing. For a few minutes, I lay like a beached sea urchin before wandering over to the other side of the island, a throwing distance and sandy all the way. As I stood there soaking it all up, I noticed a little boy liberating coconuts from a palm tree. I waved up to him, and as he waved back, I was momentarily concerned that he might fall, then I realised that it was his environment, not mine.

The handful of inhabitants I saw on the island waved and smiled as I passed them. The Kuna people were an Indian tribe who sold craftwork and caught fish for tourists. I returned to the beach and was surprised to find Daveed drinking Jack Daniels with a Kuna cross-dresser who gave me a wink. I shrugged and went off to join the others for a game of frisbee.

Unsurprisingly, I felt wholly detached while on the island, and any complications I had back home seemed irrelevant. I had a recurring feeling of looking at what was going on around me as though it was through the eyes of an alien from a different planet, enabling me to realise how too much importance is often attached to trivial subjects.

Of course, this is all relative. People all lead different and complex lives, attaching varying levels of importance to areas as they see fit, so it's easy for me to write this in the judgement of what is and is not essential. Nevertheless, from time to time, I have seen more happiness and gratitude in the eyes of kids who have nothing compared with those who have everything. And this gets me thinking about the number of things we worry about that bear no relevance to how we'll feel during our reflections in later years.

As I sat on the beach, I felt an immense surge of appreciation and was finally at peace with the horns of Cartagena. Only hours earlier, I'd kept a solitary watch as we sailed through the night to get there, occasionally tilting my head back to gaze at the crisply clear black night scattered with diamonds. My nostrils had been filled with the salty smell of the Caribbean air as its light breeze caressed my cheek. Consumed on all sides by water and darkness, I felt a connection with my maker and gave thanks for our planet.

I made a pact with myself to try and be more spiritual in the matrix of life upon my return.

I would start by honking less.

Gringo Trails - There For Good Reason

Fleur Mann, Melbourne, Australia

THE BOLIVIAN BORDER OFFICIAL STOPPED his Vespa at the side of the road and pointed to a page in my phrasebook, saying, "Quiero hacerte el amor." It meant, 'I want to make love to you.' As I sat on his old moped, I looked around to see if there was anybody to help. We may as well have been in the Sahara Desert for all it mattered. The whites of his eyes lit up against his sweaty, dark skin, set against a background of thick green jungle. He said it mischievously, and my traveller's heart sank. Not here. Not now. Not me.

I was alone, stuck with this sleazy man in one of the world's most remote regions, while he kept repeating those words. Everybody in Bolivia was a salesman, especially this border guard trying hard to flog his love life. Then, just as suddenly as he'd started the chat-up routine, he stopped. Why I still don't know. Perhaps it was a realisation that I wasn't interested, but whatever it was, we were back on the road to nowhere, and I was back wondering how I'd ended up in my predicament.

Our journey into north Bolivia's heart of darkness began a week earlier when my brother James and I abandoned the tried and tested 'gringo trail' for an off the road border crossing into Peru. We travelled from the small town of Rurrenabaque to another one in Bolivia's far northwest, Cobija. Originally touted as a 30-hour bus journey between the two, the more accurate description would have been a 'five-day torture trip'.

With passengers cramped together like fresh frogspawn, our shoddy old bus became stuck day after day on the boggy roads during the wet season. It wasn't long before we were entirely miserable that we'd come up with the idea.

We finally made it to Cobija, and after recuperating for a night, we continued with renewed determination. We headed west on another battered old bus and stopped at a hellish-looking border town, aptly named Extrema and mysteriously absent from any map we've ever checked since. Extrema is a small military jungle base that is probably used solely for extorting money from unsuspecting gringos. It looked like a total hellhole and not a place you'd ever want to spend even a single night. Of the two of us, only I spoke Spanish, so I left James with the bags and searched for a border station for permission to cross into Peru that very day.

It was here that I met the Bolivian border official for the first time. He appeared riding his battered Vespa out of nowhere and said I had to go with him. Confused, scared, and a little naive in hindsight, he drove me to a deserted outpost where an overhead fan rattled as he dropped his guns (yes, he had two) onto a desk. I was trying to remain calm, but my heartbeat was pounding in my ears louder than the chatter of the jungle's insects. As I sat with my back to the wall, he asked coldly about my reasons for wanting to cross the border. Flies were trying unsuccessfully to land on us due to the overhead fan, while my darting eyes noticed disgusting stains on the walls. My imagination ran wild, and though the answers I gave him were honest, they seemed to be coming from someone else's mouth.

He appeared convinced yet ordered that I take off my shirt for a drug search. When he saw I was 'clean', he nodded and pointed lower, unzipping his jeans to show me what he meant. Beads of sweat rolled down my back as I prayed that this was routine, and thank God when he found no hidden extras, he signalled for me to put my clothes back on.

With my adrenaline racing, I jogged back to the bus for James and our bags, telling him through short sharp breaths about where we had to go. I didn't tell him what had happened until later that day, as we already had enough on our plate. We hiked back to the same building, and the border guard was waiting for us, leaning against a wall with his hands in his pockets and a matchstick in his mouth like a shady character from a scary travel story. He looked surprised to see James but made no effort to search him for drugs. Instead, he indicated that he wanted to rummage through our backpacks.

He found a small salt alpaca wrapped in a clear plastic bag in my bag. Although we'd bought this trinket at the stunning salt flats of the Solar de Uyuni, the guard shook his head and smiled as if he'd just uncovered a drug find. We made our protests and demonstrated for him to lick it, and he did so and made a surprised laugh as though he was suddenly proud of his country's achievements in manufacturing salty alpacas.

Finally convinced that we weren't smugglers, he relaxed and said we'd need to hire a boat to reach a nearby town on the Peruvian side, down the River Madre de Dios. As he didn't speak Spanish, James was to stay behind in the office as the border official took me to find an available boat. James didn't look too pleased about the situation at first, but once the guard handed him both of the guns and told him to man the building, he shrugged and accepted his new job with a chuckle.

After we'd started our journey, the official began his translations of making love to me. Even though he didn't force himself any more than verbally, it was still one of the most uncomfortable situations I'd ever been in. As we bounced along, searching for the river, I felt the wind rushing through my unwashed greasy hair. I held onto his sweaty shirt and couldn't help thinking over and over that I was done with Bolivia.

Poor James had to wait for three of the most prolonged hours before I returned. He told me he'd begun to think the worst and had started taking short films of the border crossing offices as evidence, should they be needed. My brother is a laidback Aussie bloke, but I dread to think what he would have done to that border guard if he'd returned without me. As it turned out, we found a boat and, later that day, crossed into Peru under the eye of a most frightful lightning storm.

After reaching the other side of the river, we hitchhiked for miles to the nearest town, Puerto Maldonado, and sought out their border patrol to try and complete the last part of our challenge. We politely handed over our passports. Two foul-tempered immigration officers ranted that we'd entered their country without a passport stamp - a 'Grande problema,' they said, which didn't need much translating for James. Heartbreakingly, they ordered us to turn around and go back in the direction we'd come from. I was on the verge of tears.

They ignored our sincere and desperate apologies, but we eventually convinced them to let us call the Australian embassy in Lima, where a familiar Ozzy accent scolded us for being stupid in attempting a border crossing like that. We passed the phone over for a sympathy plea from our brothers in the capital, and for a while, it looked futile. At some point, cocktails in Lima must have been promised to someone, because not long later, our passports were stamped by a couple of cross Peruvian officials.

As we walked away, I promised myself that I would never try anything like it again. Even though it made for a great story, I'm far happier now staying firmly *on* the gringo trail.

Shampoo Liberation

Hank T. Connors, Vancouver, Canada

IT WAS ONE WEEK BEFORE Christmas, and I was on a one-way bus ticket from Foz do Iguacu to Rio de Janeiro, with no idea where I'd go after that. I was trying to be a free-spirited 1960s writer - 40 years later in a new millennium.

The ride was a punishing 27-hour journey with the sun beating relentlessly on a bus with no air-conditioning or operating windows. The passengers were the dodgiest characters you could imagine, like vagabonds from a Charles Dickens novel who seemed to be smuggling black-market goods onto the streets of Rio to sell as Christmas presents. Everyone appeared to know one another by how they shouted 100 words per second in each other's faces. At first, I took this language as a cross between Arabic, Russian and Spanish, which was strange considering we were in Brazil. This was the first time my ears were tuning into Portuguese.

A humongous giant of a man who looked like the Hothwampa monster from Star Wars led them. With a thick grey beard, a dirty white sleeveless vest and enormous arms with masses of wiry tricep hair, he wandered up and down the bus barking out instructions as though he were a general in an army. Occasionally he became irate, and the rest of the ants hid as though he were an aardvark with a cold. He tried talking to me a couple of times, but when my responses only came in Spanish, he laughed in my face.

Due to oxygen deprivation, I slept through all bar one of the rest stops and was constantly famished. All I'd brought with me was a packet of obligatory biscuits and a long since melted chocolate bar glued to the inside of my bag. During the stop I was awake for, I managed to grab the canteen's last skewer of tepid chicken and devoured it as though I'd just run a marathon. I loved that chicken so much I think I'll remember it on my deathbed.

I'd been recommended to pre-book a hotel room in Rio, as during the Christmas holidays, it gets jam-packed. I was way too blasé about this, so I was exhausted and homeless when we eventually rolled into the massive bus terminal. It was close to midnight, and the temperature was holding steady at 34 degrees.

On collecting my rucksack from the driver, I noticed that one of the shady bunch had been through it, though from first glance didn't appear to have taken anything. I did see, however, that a shampoo bottle had burst spectacularly inside. This was as welcome as a fart in a spacesuit, but it foamed a lather on my lower spine once I got walking, which was soothing.

I was exhausted from sleeping too much, eating scraps, and being exposed to animated conversations I couldn't join. But for some reason, something clicked. I'd made it to Rio in one piece, and even though I didn't know what I'd do next, I smiled and felt liberated.

Although life was challenging at that moment, I felt I'd be out of it in a couple of hours. There was shampoo leaking from the bottom of my bag and a taxi driver in my face trying to rip me off, but all I could do was smile.

I had no idea what was coming next.

ADRENALINE ADVENTURERS

A Graveyard In The Sky

Gail Honne, Austin, USA

NORTH OF BOLIVIA'S CRAZY CAPITAL La Paz, lies an infamous mountain pass called La Cumbre. Driving to it involves an Andes mountain climb up to 4,700 metres - a height universally recognised as 'very high altitude', where oxygen is in high demand but short supply. The landscape is desolate and depressing, little grows there, and death is a conqueror. The mountain peaks have a sprinkling of snow like icing sugar on rock cakes, and the clouds appear close enough to taste. The road runs down toward a small town called Coroico, 64 spectacular kilometres away and 3500 metres lower. It is considered by many to be the 'World's Most Dangerous Road' and is otherwise known as 'The Death Road' for short. I couldn't wait to cycle down it.

We woke before 6 am that morning, breakfasting on the usual sachets of decaffeinated coffee accompanied by semi-stale bread and solid butter. No matter where you went in Bolivia, breakfast was always the same and always basic, and you could tell you were in a developing country simply by the first meal of the day.

After eating, we mounted our bikes onto the top of the van, sharing nervous thoughts and reassuring one another to take it easy and that safety was paramount. We hoped that our shared fear would keep us grounded for the day. As a group, this would be our second adventure together, and our first had been a four-day hike to Peru's mighty Machu Picchu.

We drew our attention to the road's notorious reputation. 2003 had been a bad one leading up to November, including a recent appalling wreck where a local bus had toppled into a ravine. A few lucky passengers were thrown from the windows as the bus rolled, but many plummeted to their graves. Twenty bodies couldn't be reached, encased in a metal tomb at the bottom. Up to 2003, roughly 200 to 300 people died on The Death Road annually. During the summer of 1983, one bus careered into a canyon killing over 100 people. It was Bolivia's worst-ever road accident.

Surprisingly, the road wasn't as busy as we'd expected. Along with scores of fellow mountain bike riders, sporadic massive trucks were the primary traffic source. I could hear them roaring uphill but always saw them late due to the heavy dust in the air. For a road with such a reputation, you'd imagine the truck drivers would be taking it easy, yet they all seemingly had a death wish with their feet firmly planted on their accelerators. Our guide mentioned that most of them chewed coca leaves to try and keep sleep at bay, leaving them intoxicated and feeling indestructible.

So why do hundreds of people die on The Death Road each year? As vehicles pass each other, the golden rule is that all those coming downhill must pass on the outside, the opposite side they're accustomed to. This gives the downhill driver a better idea of their left-hand wheel, especially as their vehicles are left-hand drive. The margin for error is minute, and as a result, human error makes up for the most significant part of fatalities.

When larger vehicles pass one another, there's a substantial strain on the ground underneath. The road is made further weak by rain and landslides peppering it, so as two vehicles pass each other, the road occasionally gives way. Our guide showed us two areas where the road had fallen away beneath, sending whatever it was tumbling down into a ravine. And those ravines were deep. So deep in places that you couldn't see the bottom.

Other reasons included heavy fog, no railings, and the desperately muddy state at certain times of the year, causing vehicles to skid off. And of course, with it being a popular mountain bike retreat, many fatalities were the result of adventurous souls misjudging corners or losing control of their bikes. Having now ridden the road, I can see how that could happen.

We set off, and our guide stated that under no circumstances should we overtake him - he was experienced in the environment, and we weren't, simple. The first section of the road was the tarmac, where we reached our fastest day speeds at about 55-60 kilometres per hour. It doesn't sound fast if you're travelling in a car, but on a mountain bike, it feels unnatural, especially when you consider that a tyre blowout could put you over the side at any point!

After 25 kilometres, the road took on a dusty surface, and our speeds slowed as we encountered an abundance of rocks, stones and potholes. Now dotted throughout the course, we began to see crosses and gravestones to our left, marking those who'd lost their lives. It was highly unnerving.

Being a keen mountain biker, I kept up with the guide and wanted to pass him on more than one occasion but thought better of it. He knew of many dangers, and I didn't, so I maintained a safe distance. The further down the road we got, the more I found similarities with climbing, as I watched his movements to know the best route through the obstacles ahead.

At roughly 50 kilometres, his back wheel hit a rock as he was cutting across the road. I wasn't too far behind him, so I saw it rise and jerk his whole bike around to the right, throwing him off when it landed. I broke hard, locked into a skid and halted about fifteen metres behind him.

After a quick assessment, he seemed more shocked than injured. Because he'd been cutting in from left to right, he was moving away from the ledge when he landed. On any other day, he might not have been so lucky. He told me that it was the first time he'd crashed in three years of starting the tour guide job. Holding his arm and ribs, he appeared in discomfort, but he said not to mention it to the others as he did his best to battle through to the end.

Most of us reached the bottom separately due to significant gaps opening up over the 64 kilometres. One of our team members had crashed fairly heavily and sustained cuts and grazes on his elbows and knees. He was okay, though, especially when considering the alternative. We collectively gulped down cold water bottles as we high-fived and laughed at how dusty we were. It was as if we'd opened vacuum bags and emptied the contents all over ourselves.

Cycling The Death Road had been spectacular at times, but we'd done it for the shot of adrenaline it offered. I said a quiet prayer for having survived it, and we each spoke of our sadness at seeing the reminders of once adventurous souls who'd lost their lives. The road attracted riders through its dangerous reputation; only that reputation had become a tragic reality for some. My family weren't aware I was doing it, and I'm sure I wasn't the only one in the group.

On reflection, I realised how our presence wasn't helping with the safety of that road. The truck drivers worked long days, and I'm sure the last thing they wanted to see as they hit their twelfth hour was a whooping tourist tearing around a corner. It was no wonder they didn't pussyfoot around us - we were simply flies bugging elephants.

The drive back up the road proved pretty nerve-racking, especially when we passed alongside other vehicles. Each time we looked over at our neighbours, they were peering down into the hungry ravine below, hoping they weren't next on the menu. But sadly, it wouldn't be long before The Death Road claimed its next victim.

The Nepalese Crocodile Hunter

Michael Good, Melbourne, Australia

CHITWAN NATIONAL PARK IN NEPAL offers a two day 25km jungle hike that presents unparalleled opportunities to see dangerous wildlife up close. It's precisely the ridiculous travel adventure I like to sign up for, so I rewrote my itinerary to include it. In hindsight, I'm far warier of seeking out such thrills now.

The night before the hike, our guide gave a presentation about the different kinds of creatures that lived in the park. He highlighted the deadly animals that we probably would *not* come into contact with (99% probability, he reckoned), including king cobras, giant crocodiles, charging rhinos, tigers (four in the 900 km square park), and the *oversized carnivorous killer bees*! The killer bees lived in underground nests, waiting patiently for large animals to come into the area before stinging them to death and then eating them. The guide added that it only took one sting from an oversized carnivorous killer bee to kill a human, and if he was trying his best to frighten us, he did a phenomenal job.

But the best was yet to come.

He went on to add that the animal the guides feared most was the sloth bear, which incidentally is no relation to a sloth. Massively unpredictable, the sloth bear weighs in at 200kg, has a punch that can smash your face in, and a bite that can crush your bones. Despite his animated delivery, the guide said we probably wouldn't see any of these dangerous animals, and he couldn't guarantee we'd see *any* wildlife at all, so not to get our hopes up. Whispers began to circulate that perhaps we'd wasted our money.

The next day, we set off in subtropical conditions with the guide assuring us that we likely wouldn't be seeing any animals that day due to the unbearable heat.

"I'm glad I forewarned you last night," he added, making us feel he was covering his back or, more hopefully, had an excellent track record of under-promising yet over-delivering.

We didn't even see a fly during the first hour, and as expectation levels lowered, we moved from land to water and paddled canoes downstream. Minutes later, the guide turned to us and calmly requested us not to rock the boats as sometimes people fell out. He said this as we passed within spitting distance of a massive crocodile floating lazily on the water's surface just metres away. It was scary as hell.

A little while later, we pulled our canoes over to the riverbank and had our first relatively safe encounter with the jungle's wild animals. Excitement spread as we spotted monkeys, mongooses and even a sleeping rhino. Our guide's words of advice in case we were to come across any non-sleeping rhinos were,

"If they charge us… [pause for dramatic effect], chuck your stuff and run!"

Reflecting on his wise words, it was only natural that we happened upon a group of non-sleeping rhinos a half-hour later and had to 'chuck our stuff and run', quite literally for our lives! We climbed nearby trees that could hold our weight and held on tightly while our sphincters twitched and adrenaline coursed. After fifteen minutes, the rhinos became disinterested and wandered off, leaving us to fetch our bags and wonder what in the buggery was going to happen next.

Immediately following the rhino scare, we came across some fresh tiger tracks and spray, so the heat wasn't keeping the animals away no matter what the guide said. We'd have loved a discovery like these only hours earlier, but now we just prayed we wouldn't be prey.

The temperature soared way above 40 degrees at midday, and the guide said all the animals would now be sleeping. With no action for the foreseeable future, he took the opportunity to talk up the surroundings with such enthusiasm that I swear he was the Nepalese cousin of our very own dearly loved Crocodile Hunter, Steve Irwin.

We came to a mud crater with a scrawny old tree growing at a 45-degree angle from its side. There was a small cave behind the tree's long dry roots, dangling down and obscuring the mouth slightly. The guide swung down in front of it and beckoned us to, "Come and take a look at what the deer have done here," but none of us gave a shit due to the heat, so we stayed where we were, and semi observed from about ten metres away. As the guide bent down to analyse his latest find, we heard his assistant say,

"Hey, isn't that a bear print in the mud?"

Then suddenly, there was a huge bloody roar, and I mean HUGE. It was the loudest noise I'd ever heard from a living, breathing being, and panic set in big time. The guide, who was still at the edge of the cave, screamed like a little girl (he later claimed he did this on purpose - yeah, right, mate) and then bolted.

A sloth bear sleeping inside to escape the heat heard our Crocodile Hunter chatting about deer patterns, felt threatened, and decided to charge. I saw a black furry blur dart from the cave as we all turned and sprinted for our lives, again. It was the only time when I genuinely thought I could have died.

After regrouping, we heard that the bear got to within a metre of our guide before his assistant lashed it with a stick so he could get away. He later said that if the bear had caught him, he'd have been a dead man for sure. He followed that up by proudly announcing,

"It was the worst experience I've ever had in ten years of doing this job!"

Nervous near-death laughter ensued as we collectively hoped that we wouldn't see another animal during the entire trip. Sure enough, though, before the day was out, we were hiding up trees and making commando-style runs to evade more territorial male rhinos. Even the sight of a solitary bee was enough to raise the collective blood pressure of the group. Be careful what you wish for - we still had fifteen kilometres and a whole day left to complete!

Thumbs Up, If You Have Them

Artemis Cruz, Strabane, Northern Ireland

After surviving hydrospeed, the description I gave to fellow travellers went along the lines of: *'Imagine you're white water rafting and fell into dangerous rapids with just a foam float to try and stay alive on for the next hour. That, my friend, is hydrospeed.'*

And that pretty much was it, except to add that I wore two wetsuits, a wet vest, wet socks and a wet hat. When I inquired why there was so much wet attire, they told me the waters were so bitterly cold that I'd likely perish halfway through without it. Even with all of this accoutrement, I still felt on the verge of contracting hypothermia after only five minutes, and the course lasted an hour! Snow and ice from the Andes mountain range fed it, which clarified why I felt like a frozen Michelin Man bobbing down the river Trancura in Pucon, Chile.

As adrenaline activities go, this was right up there with the most bizarre. Four of us started the course, and only two of us finished - the guide and myself. The other two flat out refused to continue after ten minutes, insisting it was too dangerous and feared for their safety. It was a tad concerning to hear, especially as we had another 50 minutes. As it turned out, the first part of the course was relatively easy compared to the heavier rapids that came later, so they were justified in their hasty retreat.

The guide himself turned out to be quite the lunatic and was probably the only person in town who'd take his job. Halfway through, I noticed that one of his thumbs was missing, but I felt safer in the ignorance of not knowing the circumstances (though this didn't stop me from thinking it was down to hydrospeed). Towards the end of the course, curiosity got the better of me, and through a combination of Spanglish and thumb pointing, I asked him where his missing digit was. He opened his unearthly frog-like eyes as wide as possible before screaming and nodding over the water with a broken-toothed grin, "SIIII, HYDROSPEEEEEED!"

Even though it didn't feel possible to be shivering any more than I was, his reply gave me further chills. I detected a pride in his voice, which almost said, "Yes, I am the craziest person in this town… I only have one thumb, and everyone knows it. Now let's go and find the deadliest rapid in these gloriously warm waters!"

Putting the obscenely cold temperatures of the water and the apparent dangers to life to one side, I had immense fun navigating the rapids and giving the guide high fives after each completed section (or high fours on his part).

After returning to my hostel, the owner asked how the hydrospeed experience had been. On hearing that I'd enjoyed it and survived unharmed, he mentioned that I'd been fortunate as the previous week, a German backpacker had broken his leg on a boulder jutting out of the water. I wasn't surprised to hear it, but I'd have taken a broken leg over a lost thumb any day of the week. Thumbs helped us evolve.

The 1980s, My Favourite Decade

Brendan, UK

THE EARLY 1980S REALLY FEELS like a different millennium now. It was a time before iPods, laptops, Wi-Fi, and smartphones, where even the sight of a games console could give a 10-year-old a heart attack. While Space Invaders invaded shores and synthesisers accompanied our hair gelled to new levels, I was dreaming of what might follow the genius of the splash-proof Walkman. It was a time when the world was changing fast, and it felt a little less tainted back then, for me, at least. Before we knew it, though, we said goodbye cruel world, hello microchips (and microwave chips).

My fondest memory around this time began with a phone call to our household from my brilliant Uncle Don. He chatted with my parents before they ritually passed the phone between my brothers and me. Out of the blue, he asked if I wanted to help a friend of his, Jamie, conduct helicopter rides at a flying festival in Yeovil the next day. I agreed in a heartbeat and caught the next train from Bedford to London for an early start.

I woke to the smell of bacon and eggs wafting from Don's kitchen, and Jamie arrived at the house shortly after that. After a sensational fry-up, he and I drove to a farm where he kept his prized helicopter. On the way there, Jamie made a phone call with a mobile phone that was the size of a small briefcase. I was in awe. Looking back on it, he was an astute, ballsy businessman and one of the ways he made his living was by offering helicopter rides. I'm pretty sure he was your stereotypical 1980s yuppie!

We parked up at the farm and started the helicopter's engine so it could warm through before taking off. I stood mesmerised, watching the blades spin at an unfathomable rate, blowing our hair in all directions as we stood beneath the giant hairdryer. When it was time, we climbed in, shut the doors, put our seat belts on, and went through a few final checks. Jamie turned to me and signalled we were good to go with his thumbs up. I smiled back and did the same, thinking it was what co-pilots were supposed to do.

My young mind was doing its best to take in each tiny detail. As peacefully as a leaf blown in autumn, the helicopter rose up and up gracefully and diagonally. Objects below that once seemed substantial first grew small and then miniature. When we reached a certain height, Jamie pushed forward on his control stick (a cyclic, I learned), and we picked up significant speed. It was a long way to Yeovil, and we had plenty of miles to eat up.

I watched as thousands of lives unwound on the roads and fields below. In small-town offices and outside supermarkets, all the people had their separate trials and tribulations, their separate life agendas.

Being a stand-in co-pilot at 16 was leaving a strong impression on me. As we sped through the sky, I fell in love with the idea of flying helicopters. At the time, I didn't consider the years of dedication it would take to get there, though - oh no - up in the sky, I could hop into it as a career. As I switched between people watching and career planning, I was too young to appreciate all the years of study, practice and dedication that got someone into Jamie's seat.

A couple of times, we radioed through to Air Traffic Control to ask for clearance into a different section of air space. The significance was likely nothing to Jamie, but it was so interesting, so adult for me. I was privy to processes I hadn't even realised existed when I'd woken to breakfast that morning.

With a half-hour to go, it began to rain. It was just a drizzle but enough to hamper our visibility somewhat. I assumed Jamie would turn on windscreen wipers like a car, but the helicopter didn't have them on closer inspection. It seemed a little unconventional when we landed in a ploughed field, and he asked me to hop out and clear the windscreen! Within 60 seconds, his co-pilot was back in his seat, and we were soaring up, up and away once more.

In windy and wet conditions, we landed at Yeovil Airport, where we met up with Jamie's crew to discuss the day's plans over mugs of steaming tea. Only things didn't quite go according to plan - the high winds and rain saw to that. So instead of offering helicopter rides, we were forced to run a covered interactive stall for the day. I couldn't complain though, after all, I was only 16 and had just arrived in a helicopter! I smiled as I leaned against a tent pole, sipping my third mug of tea as I searched for the digestive biscuits. It had been one heck of a morning.

I feel such nostalgia for the 1980s that I'd gladly go back to it at the tap of a Phil Collins snare drum. Flying in Jamie's helicopter was one of many happy memories that I reflect on, and to this day, it still reminds me of how small we all are.

Amazingly, so many people weave their lives together daily without ever knowing. As the world keeps turning, everyone is the lead character in their own movie.

Get Ready For Some Shrinkage

Glen Hanoi, LA, USA

AS A BOY, I LOVED the 180-degree cinemas that took you around the world while you stood there swaying. From the lofty peak of K2 one moment to a high-speed car chase ripping through San Francisco's steep streets the next, the screen took you right to the action. For me though, the most exhilarating was being transported into a raft that was hurtling down a wild white water river towards angry frothing rapids. Back then, the Cine180 made white water rafting out to be the most fun possible for a 10-year-old. I'd spin out more than stepping off any roller coaster.

This childhood dream came true when presented with a real-life rafting opportunity in the Andes. The night before the adventure, as our rafting group stored up on carbs and wine, we openly discussed what we should expect from the river. We didn't have much experience between us and were coming up against a grade four, which meant we could expect a few 'turtle's head popping out' moments. One of our efficient Germans had done his research and broke the grading system down for us as follows:

- Grade two was for people with a heart condition (easy rider).
- Grade three was the most popular choice (not difficult, but a few jittery rapids that might successfully convert into heart attacks for the infirm).

- Grade four was a challenging course (many crap your pants moments).
- Grade five was seriously challenging (usually avoided by the standard tourist as there were very realistic chances of drowning).
- Grade six was downright dangerous (a popular choice for the deranged, and if you survived, it was more down to luck than judgement).

You may be wondering why I didn't mention grade one here? Well, from the pattern of the others, we gathered it was a bit like farting in a bathtub, so not something we needed to discuss!

After arriving at HQ, we assessed the river's immediate danger, but nothing looked intimidating. We donned our wetsuits and sat down for a briefing with the local guide, who said he'd yell the shots from the back of the raft. He'd command when to paddle forwards, backwards, slowly, quickly, when to lock our feet in and when to scream (though I think we had that one covered). We nodded that we understood, and he said it was time to let the rafting games begin.

We carried the raft to the river and walked it in between the seven of us, our spines tightening with our first steps into the icy waters. According to the strongest and weakest paddlers, we took our places and started downstream, admiring the stunning scenery. Immediate mountains loomed over us with their immense Andean brothers in the far distance, helping us to punctuate the air with appropriate "oohs" and "aahs". It was awe-inspiring, reminding us of the dramatic New Zealand backdrops from The Lord of the Rings.

Five minutes later, we came upon our first group of rapids. These would have been right at home on a grade two river, jolting us up and down harmlessly and sending a current of giggles through the raft like a group of school kids told a silly joke. Dropping into the fourth rapid, a freezing wave that doubled up as a slap in the face engulfed us. Any uncovered body parts were instantly brought to life, while any unmentionables ran for cover! The freezing waters that hit us slowly numbed our faces and fingers as we continued. At first, we didn't notice it consciously, but we touched our faces and felt nothing within a half-hour.

We reached a calmer section at two-thirds into the course, which allowed our guide to tell us a few facts. He pointed out various volcanoes and mountains, recalling their names and adding facts about heights and eruptions where possible. Our collective oohs ended when he concluded that the river was about to get "perilous" and we'd need our wits and teamwork to get through to the finish, adding that, "Any mistakes could be fatal". I'm sure he only said the last part to create more tension, but nevertheless, we prepared for a hard slog.

The rush of water grew louder until we turned a bend and saw a white rapid swirling ahead of us like a hungry frothing monster. We sat with our paddles in hand, stealing glances at one another, sharing the same nervous tension. I was back in the Cine180 all those years ago, and now I was about to live it in the flesh. Being somewhat anaesthetised by the previous rapids, we were determined to keep the raft upright and stay out of the water. We held onto our oars with a steely grip as the guide yelled his demands over Mother Nature's furious roar, "FORWARD, FORWARD! FASTER, FASTER!"

After entering the vortex, my memory of the mayhem is brief. Sitting at the back of the raft, I saw us hit the first rapid and dip what seemed like in half. The front two of our team were overwhelmed by a strong wave that quickly found its way over the rest of us. I don't think we had any control over the raft at that moment, and it certainly wasn't judgement that prevented us from flipping over, that's for sure.

Our original plan to paddle like billy-o to safety came to nothing. After being spat out the other side, our guide announced that we'd survived the most strenuous section without being flipped, so thankfully, nobody would catch pneumonia that day. Afterwards, I felt relieved that we hadn't been on a grade five river, which could conceivably have been 'fatal'.

Our team, now united in relief, paddled through to the end of the course tackling grade three rapids with new confidence and structure in our paddling technique - the big time rafters we now were. We finished the course of rapids unscathed, albeit with numbed smiles and much shrinkage for the guys.

The Cine180 is still handy for getting around the world in 15 minutes, but if you want to get hit by an icy wave as you debate your sanity, well, that's an adrenaline rush in its base form, let me assure you. There's no proper substitute for it.

DANGEROUS ADVENTURERS

A Fine Line

Anonymous

Matt wanted to experience the 'real' South America. He just didn't think it would turn out quite so authentic.

As arrests go, it wasn't the hardest investigation that the Peruvian Police Force has ever carried out. If I said it was like taking candy from a baby, then I wouldn't be giving babies enough credit.

I don't remember much of the actual arrest. Matt held up his hands on either side of his ears as an Italian footballer does after a cynical foul. I recall seeing my credit card on the window ledge, right next to our bag of charlie, and my heart, which had dropped out of my arsehole when I realised we were being arrested by military police. Oh, and they had guns. Big fuck-off ones.

"En el Carro senores," he said.

"In the meat wagon," to you and me.

As we bounced along in the back of the military jeep, we made our first couple of futile attempts to pay them off. Our $24 wouldn't have gone far between the five of them, and I'm embarrassed to say it was reminiscent of those Friday night taxi rides where you don't have enough to pay the fare, yet you clumsily try to bargain with the cabbie. We weren't kicked out a mile before our destination on this occasion.

Instead, we got to jail just after 4 am and were plonked on two wooden chairs in front of two plainclothes officers in aviation sunglasses. The spotlights were bright (but not that bright), and they looked as though they were wearing peculiar retro tracksuits and caps. The get-up made them look like Latin American versions of 1970s TV cops. They were flanked by two of the five uniforms that had picked us up earlier.

One of them made notes as the uniforms narrated the past hour's events, while I denied I could speak Spanish. The other looked familiar.

It soon turned into a standoff. They asked us to sign our statement. We refused. We asked to speak to an English-speaking lawyer before we could sign. They refused. They asked us to sign. We refused. This carried on for an hour or two. They locked us up.

I must have fallen asleep soon after and awoke to blind panic.

"You awake? We're not the only ones here you know mate. The three blokes over there reckon they're going to be here for at least a year. They got caught with a little bit of weed last month. We had charlie mate. We're fucked, aren't we? Look at that bog. This is ridiculous. Unbelievable."

Matt had been talking to the three bearded young men sharing a foam mattress in the opposite corner and was panicking. He'd calculated the amount of money he had access to and was working on the best way to offer our guards.

"I've got £4,325. Some of it's in traveller's cheques, some of it's in the bank. How much have you got? We've got to get out of here. Do something. Come on. You can speak Spanish. Speak it!"

When I asked one of the guards for a phone call, he laughed, and it sent Matt over the edge. To say he broke down would be unfair. It was more of a whimper.

"When you sign, you speak someone that speaks English."

"Get fucked," to you and me.

One of the lifers told me they always kept you in until they had the results of a blood test. That way, they could see if you had drugs in your system. This would take two weeks, as samples travelled to Lima and back. I didn't translate for Matt. He was having difficulty with two hours behind bars. I hoped they would put me in solitary.

The morning became the afternoon, and the two guards became five again. A card school kicked off around the desk, and someone who looked like a Chief arrived, aviation sunglasses and all. He looked familiar too.

"Listen, guys," said the Chief. "We need to go to the hospital, check some things with the doctor; look at your blood. Know what I mean?"

The bribes were mounting up. The Peruvian Starsky and Hutch, the uniforms, the Chief, the Doc. £4,325 wasn't going to be enough. Matt looked thoughtful. Maybe he was considering re-mortgaging his grandmother's house in Nottingham.

As we hadn't actually had a single conversation with anyone, our imaginations were doing overtime. At best, we thought we were joining the lifers on their foam mattress, although we'd need one of our own as there was no way all five of us would fit on theirs. At worst, we were taking a trip up to Lima. The Chief still looked familiar.

It was on the way to the hospital that he told us they wanted to make us an offer. We weren't hopeful. Our friends back in the jail cell had got us thinking in terms of jail, but we were asked if we wanted to listen to their offer. Matt bit his hand off.

It was good news. The Chief would help us with our 'problem'. He would speak on our behalf while they tested the powder, tested our blood and took a statement from us. It could go well, or it could go badly. Some $400 would make sure that it went well. Matt was gnawing at the elbow.

We arrived at the clinic, and the doctor had a warm greeting for us all. I think they had been expecting us, or someone like us. Blood samples were taken. The tests were handled quickly and quietly before a trip to another police building (via a quick stop at a cash point) for a statement to be re-written in English.

The tests were found to be negative, the charlie had turned into Aspirin, and everyone turned into each other's best friend.

"We are very sorry about the confusion, gentlemen," said Mr Sunglasses.

"I am sure you understand that we need to follow procedures. Peru is a very complicated country. You are free to go."

It took us a while to work it all out. The Chief must have got his new pair of Raybans. The Uniforms got some new uniforms. The Doc got his weekend away with the wife, and maybe even the lifers got a new mattress. $400 goes a long way in Peru.

The guy that sold us the stuff in the first place was probably still right outside Bar Cuzco, where all the trouble had started. It had been busy there, and we'd been lucky to get in, given we were already wrecked. The guys on the door gave us the benefit of the doubt, though. Nice guys, actually.

I just couldn't understand why they were wearing dark aviation sunglasses at one o'clock in the morning...

Children, Avoid Jail

Bobby Ahn, Austin, USA

THE DAY BEFORE MY 21ST birthday, I had to renew my driver's licence at the Department of Motor Vehicles in Austin, Texas. It was a mundane but necessary task to keep my freedom.

After waiting for an hour, the clerk informed me that a state trooper wanted to speak to me, so he led me into a room where the trooper said I was being charged with a Class C misdemeanour, but he had no further information. I protested my innocence while he put me in handcuffs and took me out the back door for a little ride downtown. Along the way, he started a one-way conversation about how spending the time arresting me was keeping him from 'going out there to get the real felons.'

I wondered what I could have possibly done to elicit such a response from the government. I couldn't think of anything, but I figured as I didn't have anything to do that afternoon, the experience of getting booked at the police station would probably make for an exciting story later (wink).

From what I knew about jail, I figured that they'd probably hold me for a Class C misdemeanour for a few hours before being released on bail. After getting checked in at the Hotel des Criminales, I sat in the tank with about ten others, and the guy next to me started a conversation about why he was there. He was a drunk driver who had quite a history of drunk driving by the sounds of it (he couldn't remember how many times he'd been in that particular tank).

After a while, I grew impatient with the whole process and asked the guards what was happening. They didn't respond. Finally, a deputy led us to another room with ten brown paper bags. He instructed us to strip completely, place our clothes in the paper bag and stand to attention as he came down the line looking each of us over. There was something terrifying about being naked and having a big guy with a baton looking you over.

We were issued our prison greys and led individually down to our cells. The cell was small, about 8 x 10 feet, with one bunk bed, of which someone occupied the lower level. My new acquaintance, Drunk Driver, was lying on a thin rollout mattress on the floor, and he seemed happy to see me. I pulled myself up to the top bunk, and a little while later, they added a fourth person. The only space left was *underneath* the bottom bunk, so he laid out his mattress and became the first level of three human shelves.

When I'd entered the cell, I'd wondered why the top bunk was vacant, and I'd also wondered why Drunk Driver had taken the floor instead. It hadn't occurred to me that the lights in the Austin jail would never go off, so being on the top bunk meant that the light shone continuously, about two feet from my face. Needless to say, I didn't get much sleep in jail!

Time is an unknown quantity to the temporary residents of Austin jail. Since you have none of your possessions, you can't do anything except think or talk to your cellmates. By now, I'd learned that the guards didn't respond to any calls, and I wondered if the moment that had just passed was ten minutes, an hour or several hours, as I couldn't be sure. The doors from the other cells and cellblocks were constantly opening and closing, letting the screams and cries of the slightly less stable escape now and then.

Finally, a guard called my name and asked me to step outside. I was handcuffed to about twenty other prisoners in a chain gang and led to an arraignment hearing where a judge read our charges and set bail amounts. I was surprised to hear that my charge was for theft by cheque. The judge said that I was to be released on my recognition and ordered me to appear in court at a later date to settle the matter. Couldn't they have mailed me a notice about it? I would have appeared in court, and the state trooper who'd arrested me could have been 'going out there to get the real felons.' Despite the flaw in the system, I was glad the ordeal was almost over.

The cheque in question was one I'd written for a haircut during my freshman year in college. The cheque bounced after I closed the account and moved back to my parent's place, so by not leaving a forwarding address, the problem hadn't caught up with me until now.

As we were led back to our cells, I glanced at a guard's watch and saw it was nearly 9 am. I'd been in jail for *18 hours*, and it was now officially my 21st birthday.

Back in the cell, I made small talk with Drunk Driver and also the guy in the bunk underneath me. I'll call him Gangsta because that's what he was. He told me various stories about his illegal activities, but I can't recall which one he was in jail for at that particular time. The other guy, Wife Beater, didn't say much. My only recollection of him talking at all was when he told us why he was there in the first place. By this time, I was known as College Boy.

As the hours passed, I began wondering what was taking them so long to process the paperwork and get me out. During the first 24 hours, the guards opened all cell doors twice, but not those to the cell block itself. This allowed us to take a short walk to get the blood circulating and make a phone call to the outside world. As the phone didn't accept money, all calls had to be collect, so I called my roommates to fill them in and also to get an update on the time. They didn't seem concerned that I'd not been home the night before, but they were concerned that I wouldn't get out in time to celebrate my birthday.

Many of the clubs and bars on Austin's Sixth Street would serve a complimentary drink to anyone who was turning 21. The bars liked it because for the cost of one drink, they could sell many drinks to their friends, and the friends liked it because they didn't have to buy anything for the birthday person. It was already past noon, but I felt sure that I'd be out to collect my free drinks by nightfall.

Later that day, I was surprised to hear my name again when the guards rounded up inmates for another arraignment hearing. Gangsta was also called. I tried to tell a guard that I'd already been through this, so it must be a mistake. He told me to shut up.

Before the judge called my name, he'd charged a man with assault on an officer and set his bail at $15,000. Then he called me. He said my charge was running a stop sign on my bicycle and that they could limit the sentence to time served. Every prisoner on the chain gang started laughing, and then Gangsta called out from the end,

"Yo, College Boy, you in here on a bicycle ticket?!"

Now that this was out, I didn't much fancy my chances in jail.

During my sophomore year of college, I'd lived close enough to the University of Texas campus to ride my bicycle to class. There was a stop sign that most cyclists would ignore along the route as you could easily turn and stay in the bike lane without crossing any automobile traffic.

One day, the police decided to set a trap for the cyclists, and as I turned the corner, I was greeted by two officers who told me to stand in a line while a third wrote out tickets for all us lawbreakers. Other than the inconvenience, I didn't think it was a big deal as I knew that the first ticket written by the

University Police was only a warning. In fact, many students walked away, tearing up their tickets.

Unfortunately, that afternoon in court, I found out to my detriment that the ticket hadn't been written by the University Police but rather by the Austin Police Department. To this day, I find the idea of three Austin police officers writing tickets for bicyclists somewhat asinine. After all, they could have been doing something much more critical like 'going out there to get the real felons.'

The guards fed you three times a day, and like everything else in jail, the meal came in a brown paper bag. No matter the time of day, it was always the same thing: a baloney sandwich, a bag of chips and a paper cup filled with watered-down grape punch. After lunch, Drunk Driver gave me an unsolicited compare and contrast of the different jails he'd seen, and it sounded like Austin jail scored on the low side. One of the jails he mentioned had way better meals.

Later, they called Gangsta's name and handed him a brown paper bag. He began shouting excitedly as he rummaged through it,

"I'm going to County bitch! YEAH! I'm going to County!"

Gangsta had been in jail for five days and was now being transferred to County Prison, a relative paradise. As he told us of the perks this brought, he pulled different items from the brown paper bag. He showed us a comb and a bar of soap, to which I thought, whatever, but then he produced a toothbrush, and that got my attention. I'd experienced the feeling of not brushing my teeth for a whole day on camping trips before, but I saw cleaning them as something of a chore even then. Now, as I touched the fur on my teeth with my tongue, brushing them would feel enormously refreshing and help break the endless monotony.

"You can even watch TV at County," he beamed. I told Gangsta he was lucky. Then I realised I'd just told someone they were lucky because they'd get to watch TV in prison. I had to get the hell out of jail. My views on reality were becoming skewed. What was taking so long?

The next time we were allowed to take a walk around the cellblock, an enormous inmate approached me. Let's call him Big Guy. He was almost six and a half feet tall and just as wide. He could have blocked the sun for several people at the beach or even provided a wind block for polar bears. He mumbled something, but it was difficult to understand his low voice and unfamiliar slang. I stepped back as he stepped forward. I looked behind me and was fast running out of real estate before I'd hit a wall. I felt that if I tried to hit Big Guy, his body would only absorb my fist, and I'd get my arm stuck. Thankfully, Gangsta came to my aid.

"Yo, leave College Boy alone, he alright," he said, to which Big Guy mumbled something. "He said he wants your dinner," Gangsta said. "No problem," I replied. It's remarkable how quickly you lose your appetite for baloney sandwiches and crisps in jail, especially when Big Guy wants them. I was happy to spend the rest of my jail time on the top bunk in the cell.

When finally released, I stepped onto Seventh Street and saw the nightlife crowd bar-hopping in vibrant Austin. I went to a payphone to see if one of my roommates might be home to pick me up, but they were all out celebrating my birthday, so I took a cab back to the DMV to pick up the car.

I drove home and stopped for cigarettes along the way, even though I'd quit years before. Back at my place, I sat on the stairway to my second-storey duplex, checked my watch, and it was 1 am. I'd spent just under 36 hours and my entire 21st birthday in jail.

I lit a cigarette and took a deep drag. Freedom. I could taste it again.

Most Wanted

Nigel Noah, Sydney, Australia

SLEEPING IN A SHARED DORM room has one major drawback – you're sharing a room with random people you've never met before. Your latest roommate could be harbouring any deep, dark secret, and you'd never be any the wiser. And sometimes, it's better not to know.

After history's most uneventful night in an allegedly haunted hostel, where the only chills were due to broken heaters, my friends Sheldon, Andy and I decided to find pastures new. In the heart of Melbourne, we checked into a respectable modern establishment, and on entering our new room, we greeted our only other roommate, a jittery Australian guy in his mid-30s calling himself Ron.

Although Ron was the only person we could see, clothes were scattered across all six beds, making us believe we'd been given the keys to an overly subscribed room. Ron assured us that we were in the right place when we questioned it, half-heartedly apologising for its poor state and gathering his clothes like a lazy teenager.

I began to unpack and asked if anyone minded me putting on a CD. Sheldon and Andy were keen, but Ron didn't reply. I took it as a sign that he wasn't fussed, but as soon as the first song started, he fired over with, "No! Stop that! Turn it off. I don't want to listen to music. I don't want to listen to anything. I am trying to *THINK*." He said the last part with a pained look on his face as he held the back of his hand to his forehead. Judging by the look on his face, he had a headache, so understandably music wouldn't help. It wasn't a big deal, but the way he responded was definitely off centre, so I placed the CD Discman to one side and told him no worries.

As I began to unpack my rucksack, I couldn't help but notice Ron moving his belongings around his bed in a severe and particular manner, almost as though he had OCD. Whether or not Sheldon saw him doing the same thing didn't stop the confident Canadian from trying to start a little friendly banter.

"So Ron, where are you from, mate?"

With his eyes half-closed, Ron raised his head, put one palm against his forehead, and held the other out as though he was trying to stop traffic. He did a brilliant job if he was trying to cut Sheldon off at the knees because no more words left my friend's mouth.

"STOP, alright! I am trying to *THINK*," he said.

Sheldon, Andy and I looked at each other with wide eyes and raised eyebrows, silently saying, "What the hell was that all about?" In unison, we looked back at the Australian who'd gone straight back to rearranging his belongings without missing a beat. Something was amiss.

Five minutes later, Ron must have wrestled free of his thoughts because he came out with a question that surprised us.

"So mate, where have you been to in Australia then?" He asked Sheldon.

"Well. We got into Melbourne yesterday. Straight from Adelaide," Sheldon replied. Just as he said 'Adelaide', Ron put both hands up to his face and began to sob.

"Hey man, are you ok?" Sheldon asked.

"It's ok; I'm getting over it. I'm dealing with it. *ALRIGHT*!"

After round three of eyeball swapping, I said, "Right, lads, I've got to go. Things to do, places to see, pictures to take, you know how it is," to which the others pretty much jumped onto the bandwagon. We needed to get away from that room fast. As we left, the atmosphere hung heavy, and as the door closed behind us, it sealed like a tomb.

For the next few hours, we discussed the bizarre behaviour of our new roommate, coming to the naturally *illogical* conclusions that young minds do. We deduced that he'd either been thrown out of his house by a partner, was experiencing the downside of powerful drugs, or was just plain old crazy. If we stayed on the right side of him, we just hoped he wouldn't perforate us in our sleep with a screwdriver.

Later in the evening, we returned to find Ron in the middle of the floor, cranking out some press-ups. As soon as we walked in, he jumped to his feet as though we'd just caught him doing something naughty. His welcome home gesture was then to start punching the lockers in the corner of the room!

"Are you ok, mate?" asked Andy, a polite, well-spoken and completely non-threatening Englishman.

"Don't *you* bloody ask *me* if *I'm* ok. Who do you think you bloody well are, hey? Piss off and mind your own bloody business," he snapped back.

At that point, I piped up. Even if Ron did have all his issues, he didn't need to be an arsehole to us, especially as we'd only ever been polite towards him, so I pointed this out. Once more, his attitude changed all too quickly as he half-heartedly apologised before wandering out of the room. The three of us had gone to sleep within the next hour, and Ron was still off wandering.

They had designed the room with three separate bunk beds. From my bed, I couldn't see Ron, and he couldn't see me, but we could both see the guys in the other bunk, and there were only the four of us sharing the room. The guys later told me that they'd both woken at different times during the middle of the night to find Ron staring directly at them with huge wide eyes!

At 4 am, I needed to take a leak. When I re-entered the room, Ron stood on the other side of the door, blocking my path. He was smoking a cigarette in a no smoking building, which wasn't exactly the biggest shock, but his glazed, blood-shot eyes were open as wide as they'd go, plus they had a crazed look.

"Bloody hell mate, what are you thinking?" I said. "You scared the shit out of me."

Nothing came back. He barged past me and stomped down the corridor as though I was the man who wasn't there. After this last act, I climbed into bed and pretended to sleep for the remainder of the night, keeping one eye slightly open. I decided that when morning came, I would persuade Sheldon and Andy that we needed to find a safer joint.

At 6 am, I watched Ron turn his rucksack upside down and scatter its contents around the middle of the room. He then repacked it slowly and clinically, finally lifting it onto his back. His final act was to let rip with a hefty stinking fart and then pirouette on his heels and walk straight out the door. I wasn't ready to start punching the air just yet, so I waited half an hour before walking over to tap Sheldon on the shoulder. He had his back to the room and was facing the wall, but from the way he replied in a clear, focused voice, it was apparent he'd been awake for hours.

"Has that cracked-up bastard left yet?" he asked.

I told him exactly what I'd seen, and it visibly lifted him. I looked to Andy's bunk above, but it was empty. We eventually found him downstairs in the television room, wrapped tightly in a blanket. When we told him that Ron was gone, you could see the immediate relief on his face too. It had all been too much for him when he woke to find Ron's crazy eyes fixed upon him during the middle of the night, so he'd crept downstairs to preserve life.

We remained in the same dorm room, Ron never returned, and people enjoyed hearing our story. Then a couple of days later, Sheldon and Andy left, and out of the blue, the police came looking for our old roommate (their station was next door to the backpackers, so they didn't have far to walk). They asked a few questions about his erratic behaviour, and when they'd finished, I asked one of my own.

"So, are you able to tell me why you're after him?" I asked.

"Sorry, we can't disclose that information," the police-woman replied.

I decided to try a more light-hearted approach. "Aaaahh, come on. At least give me something. We had to endure his crazy behaviour for 24 hours and feared for our safety."

She looked to her superior, who gave a harmful nod as though bidding for a potential lead.

"Well, at this moment, your old roommate *Rod* is one of Australia's top ten most-wanted criminals. We need to talk to him about an actual bodily harm incident and the theft of a truck in Adelaide," she replied, looking at me in the faint hope that it might jog my memory. It didn't.

After the police left, I sat back and reflected on the whole story as though it was the end of a thriller I was now piecing together. His insecurities, his erratic state, the random outbursts, yes, they were all evidence of a man on the run. Then I remembered the breakdown he had. It must have been because of the pain of hearing the word *Adelaide*. But why had he only changed one letter in his name? Going from *Rod* to *Ron* was hardly going to throw the cops off the scent. Whatever the outcome, though, I was left thinking that sharing a dorm room with a top ten most-wanted criminal would make for a decent story somewhere down the line.

As I sat in a library some 1,200 miles north in Queensland, a phone call came through on my mobile six weeks later. The caller was a detective from the Victoria *Homicide* Department wanting to ask a few questions about Rod. After we finished, he disclosed that they'd caught him, but only after a televised high-speed chase where he'd tried to get away in another stolen truck. Once in custody, Rod was charged with committing a hefty crime the day before we met him - murder! I was blown away. Totally flabbergasted. Now when I look back on it, we'd been witnessing one man's emotional fallout to committing a murder.

The detective finished off the conversation by saying they'd potentially need me as a character witness in the trial, and they'd be willing to pay for my travel to get there. When I told him I was headed to South America later that year, he must have had second thoughts about the price of trans-Pacific flights, though, because the call never came.

So, this story concludes that you never honestly know who you're sharing a backpacker dorm room with. The guy in the next bed could be a millionaire, a regular dude, or if you're really unlucky, a total nut job.

After hanging up with the detective, I looked to the heavens and thanked my lucky stars for a fortunate escape. Then I turned to the old guy sat next to me and said,

"Hey mate, do you want to hear a good story?"

Student Adventures

Lee Henaghan, Nelson, New Zealand

IRRESPONSIBLE STUDENT BEHAVIOUR ISN'T UNUSUAL. It's probably fair to say you're even expected to do some downright stupid, half-witted shit in the three years it takes you to blag yourself a degree. In my case, I didn't make it past the halfway point of the second year, but in that relatively short space of time, I pulled off a few stunts that make me thank my lucky stars I'm still breathing.

One that stays with me was a fiasco that began on a cold rainy night in October 1999. Like all my other ridiculous decisions, it started with a flash of inspiration and a complete overestimation of my skills and talent.

For three weeks running, the newly installed halogen security light in our back garden had been burning night and day. Brought in by our landlord to improve security, it came on when someone stepped into the garden and then switched itself off when they left. However, like most things in a house containing six guys, it didn't quite work properly. Day and night, the light stayed on.

At first, we laughed it off. Then, we even welcomed it when our new 24-hour glow gave us all ringside seats for a three-way feline gangster rumble one Saturday night. Nevertheless, it soon dawned on us that the perma-noon in our back yard was costing us a small fortune in electricity bills. And it goes without saying that when you're a student, any hair-brained scheme to save a few quid instantly becomes attractive.

After an extensive, fruitless search for a plug or switch, the only physical link we could find between the mains power supply and the lamp outside was a thick black cable running down the brickwork. It didn't take an Einstein to figure out that cutting the wire would solve our problem, and Einstein, I most definitely was not!

Now that's not to say I didn't apply a certain amount of scientific theory. I knew neither wood nor rubber conducted electricity, so I felt safe assuming that a pair of marigold washing up gloves and a sturdy wooden-handled kitchen knife would be all the protection I'd need against the 300 odd volts running through the cable.

I stepped into the garden, being egged on by my housemates, who were only too aware of the life-threatening scrape I was about to get myself into. I hadn't considered that they'd probably decided long ago that the £3.37 we'd save in energy bills each month would make this worthwhile.

Unsure whether to go for a slow sawing action or a one-off chop, I began to have second thoughts, but it was too late. I'd come too far down the line to turn back now. The next thing I knew, I was lying a full six feet away, thrown onto the grass by an explosion. I lay dazed and confused, staring up at the night sky. When I got my bearings back, I looked over to see my housemates laughing so much that they could barely speak.

Still shaking, I rose to my feet and looked down at the life-saving equipment. The Marigolds were warm and blackened with residue, but there was a two-centimetre gap in the edge of the kitchen knife where the current had melted the blade. After a while spent wondering why I hadn't shut the house power off at the mains, I slowly but surely began to see the funny side.

Looking back now, it reminds me that shows like 'The Young Ones' weren't that farfetched after all. Let's face it; some crazy, foolish, straight-up nutty adventures have been going on in student houses worldwide for decades.

And long may they continue.

War Memories

Mike Lunness, Stevenage, UK

AS I SAT WATCHING THE TV programme commemorating the sixtieth anniversary of the D-Day landings, the years rolled back, evoking memories of a schoolboy's war. I know the first few years are generally believed to be the most formative, but I consider the war years to be when I learned the most.

I was just seven years old when Britain declared war on Germany in 1939. They were years of happy days, roaming fields, birds nesting, trying to catch mythical fish and camping underneath bright stars. Although our happiness was mixed with disruptive schooling, nights of apprehension, and sleeping in an air-raid shelter, there was a great sense of adventure shared by boyhood pals who are now scattered in unknown places.

The government's Anderson shelters were available to everyone for free. When they arrived, an immense excitement spread through our neighbourhood as we inspected the large sheets of curved corrugated steel, brightly galvanised and gleaming in the sunlight. Families and neighbours joined forces by digging them into the ground and bolting them together, an act that produced a great sense of solidarity amongst Britain's citizens. It was almost snug with a concrete floor and four half-height internal walls. We had to scurry *down* our air raid shelter - it was three quarters buried into the garden. Banks of earth covered the outside, and several of the neighbours finished theirs off with flowerbeds, potted plants or shrubs, depending on their artistic whims. Father's category was undecided; he was talking survival. A layer of railway sleepers covered ours, and a direct hit would have bounced the bomb back to Hitler in Germany.

Years of wartime nights were spent tucked up inside that shelter. We slept serene, ignoring sirens and only waking when things became close or desperate, kitted out with bunks and blankets. As we grew older and bolder, we stood on top of the shelter observing aircraft, searchlights and flames in an eerie atmosphere of smoke and muffled noise. What kinds of bombs were being dropped? How near to us were they? What type of aircraft was above us? These were questions that never grew dreary.

Blasé we may have become, but I'll never forget sitting with tight fists and a wisp of fear as deafening explosives whistled down around us, rocking our shelter and making my young siblings cry. Our house stood at the centre of a group of potential targets, including the power station, the railway yards, and four large factories. Around us, we had anti-aircraft gun sites operated by the army and barrage balloon sites handled by the RAF. We sat around their fires some evenings, listening to masculine tales while inspecting their guns with awe. Occasionally, a couple of girlfriends turned up to promote a great singsong with their accordions, sending us happily off to another night in the shelter.

Catching sight of the barrage balloons on fire was always a time of excitement. If the balloons were up in a storm, their metal cables served as dangerous lightning conductors, so it was imperative to get them down. When struck by lightning, a burning balloon fell like an old Zeppelin with flaming fragments showering hazardously around it. In an austere world of rationing, a large piece of barrage balloon was a grand prize; in fact, my first canoe was covered in balloon fabric. Barrage balloons occasionally broke loose during high winds, taking off erratically across the rooftops with gangs of youngsters following eagerly, gasping at each crashing tile and chimney pot. Trudging home hot and flushed after a long chase was always satisfying.

Most of the large factories had their own fire brigade, and my father was the fire chief at *Lawrence & Scotts*, who had about 40 men and 10 Coventry Climax pumps to assist them. It seemed like he was forever at the fire station or off fighting fires back then. During the Blitz, he and his crew spent upwards of a week continuously fighting the devastation in London. They'd arrive back covered in black grime, desperate for a hot bath and a good night's sleep. Then they'd leave to do it again a few days later. Later in the war, my father also qualified as a bomb disposal officer, such was the need for people to turn their hands to different jobs. When they searched for unexploded bombs with steel rods in the early days, it was pretty difficult for them to tell a bomb from a gas pipe!

While my brave father was off trying to repair our country, we kids were never at a loss for mischief. War or no war, I'm sure we'd have been the same, but there were never-ending possibilities for tomfoolery during this period.

On occasion, we interrupted Home Guard exercises by giving away defenders' hiding places to the attacking forces, though they didn't like it. Within our neighbourhood, walls and passages intersected our houses' backs, making it too easy for a quick getaway during moments like these. I'd vanish down an alley, scale a couple of walls and be home before anyone had realised where I'd gone. I'd scamper into the house and ask my mother if she had any jobs where she needed help.

"Why don't I peel the potatoes?" I'd ask as if I was an angel sent to help, and then I'd stand at the sink innocently, waiting for the dreaded and inevitable knock on the door.

"Where's your Michael? He's been up to no good, I say!"

"Not my boy, he's been here peeling my potatoes with me," Our Gladys would reply.

The evening would creep in, bringing the irritated neighbours to complain to a higher power. Father, whose judgment may not have been as wise as Solomon's, could deliver a swift and terrible punishment. My mother, who was hassled on all sides by demanding siblings, would protest my innocence. Shame I feel now, but not then. Then it was fear. My mother, Our Gladys, was a saint worthy of two others. She left me good skin, rose-coloured spectacles to view the world, a love of family, and everlasting gratitude. Without a doubt, we were rapscallions, and I admit to mischief, skylarking and (grudgingly) to nuisance, but we were never wicked or malicious.

We explored everything, everywhere, even bombed homes with their dust-covered belongings scattered far and wide. Stupidly we'd sneak into the store at the Lansdowne Hotel, requisitioned as headquarters for the army's bomb disposal squad. Climbing through the side window, we'd take handfuls of bullets, break them open and use the cordite to make experimental rockets and fireworks. It wasn't a very secure bomb store!

Practice firebombs, used by the fire service to simulate incendiary bombs, were thrown into tin sheds filled with old furniture to create a contained inferno. Firefighters donned breathing gear to practice putting fires out as we sat around watching, enthralled. One Sunday, our gang discovered a practice firebomb that hadn't ignited (in theory, a gigantic firework). Bullseye, it was ours. After a secret struggle to dry it out, the day arrived for us to test our weapon. Late one afternoon, a small group of us set out for Carey's Meadow, a quiet place where we knew we wouldn't be disturbed by adults. We hid our prize inside a jacket, protected from the damp air. Bravely clutching a box of Swan Vesta matches, we crossed the railway lines into the meadow and began a series of unsuccessful attempts at lighting our bomb.

Becoming disheartened with the weather, the discarded broken matches, and the fast-approaching darkness, we huddled in for one last effort. Before we had the chance to get excited, there was a WHOOSH followed by a blinding flash. Waves of panic overcame us as we ran from the scene. My heart thumped through my chest, and breaths came in short gasps. The intense white light lit up the whole field, throwing distorted shadows in front of our faces, adding to the unanimity that we'd gone too far this time. We were scared stiff and vanished like startled rabbits in the railway-shunting yard between goods wagons. All of this was an hour before blackout when any chink of light incurred furious wrath from the air raid wardens. We got away with it, and the story became legend.

The fears and worries that beset our parents during the war did not reach down to us. We enjoyed our organised chaos, especially when our school was raised to the ground with one direct hit from a bomb. Imagine having endless school holidays with your friends - that was us.

Norwich had 35,569 houses. 2,082 houses were destroyed, 2,651 were seriously damaged, and 25,621 were moderately damaged. This means that 30,354 out of 35,569 were affected - roughly six-sevenths. Can this be true? If so, how could I have enjoyed it?

A thousand tales to be told, the past is dead, and time will erase all memories.

COURAGEOUS ADVENTURERS

Two Conversations

Pete Sebastian, New Malden, UK

"I AM A VERY STRONG MAN".

Tilak was working out. His bedroom doubled as a gym with just two pictures on the wall: a large picture of him and an equally large picture of the Empire State building. He had never left Nepal except to visit India and was fascinated to hear that I'd been to New York many times. I enjoyed telling him what it was like, a small connection to the world that I'd left a train ride, two flights and a four-hour motorcycle trip behind.

I was not working out. The 40-degree heat made me sweat profusely, so I didn't feel I needed to. Tilak had been lifting weights for fifteen minutes while I watched, and already I'd sweated more than him.

I'd been in Nepal a month, and I felt old. It would've been cool to shower in cold rainwater collected in a bucket overnight in my early twenties. I wouldn't have minded regular power cuts, 'load shedding' from Nepali electricity companies who don't have enough power to stay on all the time. And waking up after a night sleeping on the floor wouldn't have felt like I'd just lost a fight. Now in my late twenties, I was hallucinating about the comforts of home. After a month of eating dal and rice for every meal, if someone had offered me the chance to buy a pizza for a thousand pounds, I would've bought it.

"We must go to work now", Tilak said. "Big day today. I have been selected from many Nepali people for a very special job at the United Nations. You will help me get this job".

Tilak was a big deal around here. While most Nepali men were short and wiry, he was six feet with a big build. I had been in many meetings with him and had played the 'who's in charge game' to help me pass the time, given that I understood minimal Nepali. Around here, grey hair and wrinkles denoted authority, and despite Tilak having neither, he always seemed in control. And he was paid to be: Tilak was the second most senior person at Backward Society Education or BASE, a Nepali charity.

BASE was royalty in Tulsipur. And Tilak's boss was King. Dilli Bahadur Chaudhary had set up BASE when he was 17, a response to seeing his father beaten and his mother raped on their own farmland simply for trying to leave to get an education. Dilli, like Tilak, was a member of the low caste Tharu community, many of whom had been cheated out of their own land by higher caste Nepalis. Dilli had given BASE an English name because he didn't think his own countrymen would donate to his cause.

And it had worked. For the last 30 years, Dilli had brought the United Nations, the World Bank and many other international organisations to his hometown. As he said to me, "people have tried to kill me many times. Life presents many challenges, you just have to work through them."

Tilak smiled a lot. And he committed to those smiles, especially when discussing Dilli, himself, his work and his family. We ate both of our daily meals together at a local hotel;

three meals was an extravagance most people couldn't afford. I found out that while he mostly worked in Tulsipur, his wife and two young children lived in Nepalgunj on the Indian border, a few hours away. There his house was large and reminded me of a Spanish holiday villa, his reward for a career helping people out of poverty.

But Tilak wanted more. And after we'd walked to the office, read the local newspapers, had tea with his staff and discussed the day's news, he was ready to take care of business.

"I have received a very great honour. I've been invited to apply for a very great job at the UN."

"That's great", I said. "What do you need to do?"

"A very great honour. I must go to Kathmandu".

"That's it? You've been invited for an interview already? When did you apply for this job?"

Tilak put his hand on my shoulder. He smiled again. His standard response to my questions,

"You see Peter? Look at this!"

He opened his email. BAN KI-MOON HAS CHOSEN YOU TO WORK AT THE UNITED NATIONS.

"The UN Secretary-General himself has emailed me!" Tilak looked at me. "What should I do now?"

Tilak was only three years older than me. But in Nepal, that mattered. Since I'd arrived, I'd been asked for help many times. Each time I suggested something, and each time I saw nothing happen. As my Nepali improved slightly, I realised later that changes were being made, albeit slowly. Tilak, and others, needed a few days to think about my suggestions and then pass them off as their own.

Now, as I stared at the email from bankimoon@yahoo. com, I had a choice; a full day working on Tilak's response to this email or telling him it was spam. The latter response would land me a whole day drinking tea outside with his staff while he processed my response. And that's what I did.

It had been two years since I'd seen Tilak. He beamed as he put his hand on my shoulder. "Great to see you!"

He'd always dressed like a PE teacher. Trainers, cream khaki trousers and a polo shirt. The uniform had remained.

"Look up! Peter, can you see? There's the Empire State Building!"

When we spoke in Nepal, I never thought he'd get here. Standing on Broadway should've felt commonplace to me. But as I stood next to my companion from the most remote experience of my life, it was me, not him, that felt out of place.

"Let's have a drink, Peter. So much to talk about."

Sitting ten blocks from the UN headquarters, I asked Tilak everything. He told me that he'd quit BASE. His family had not come with him to America, and I wasn't sure if they were still in their house, but he couldn't afford to bring them over at the moment. He had no job and no valid visa to stay in the country, from what I could work out. He'd come over to stay with a friend, but he couldn't last long in his current place.

"Tilak, are you ok? And your family?"

He looked at me, leaned in, and smiled.

"Peter, I'm in the United States. This is the biggest opportunity of my life."

A few minutes later, he was off, striding into the crowds. Just before he disappeared, I took a picture to record the moment. We've not spoken since.

Five years have passed since I took that picture. When I found it again, I decided to see what had happened to Tilak. He's now living in Chicago with his family. I found a picture of him wearing Oakley glasses, driving a big American car, staring straight ahead.

Big Mexican Cajones

Ian White, UK

DURING THE BALMY SUMMER OF 1986, I was besotted with the Football World Cup in Mexico. They were the days of short shorts, Gary Lineker goals, Maradona playing the anti-hero role, and a mascot called Pique doubling up as a chilli pepper during his day job. For me, though, the best part was watching those fantastic waves circulating the ground time and time again. It was the first Mexican wave I ever saw, and I fell in love.

Fast-forward 17 years, and I'm now a grown man with tickets to watch England play their first-ever match in Leicester, my home city. It was only a friendly against Serbia & Montenegro, but the national team had never visited Leicester in my lifetime, so fever pitch was in the air.

That night, I ran home from work, pulled on my England jersey, and bounded off towards the stadium with my infamous friend Mad Ash, a grown man with the cheekiness of a child. En route, we discussed Mexican waves and whether we might see one that evening. We'd seen them at Leicester matches before, but this was different. We'd be watching England live for the first time, and it felt like another time and place.

Closer to the ground, the crowd resembled an army picking up new soldiers on its way to a battlefield. Wherever the eye focussed, colours meshed together. White shirts, blue scarves and red flags mixed with blue shirts, white flags and red scarves. Children with painted faces smiled as they ate hot dogs and swigged from fizzy pop bottles. They'd remember this night for years, just as we had from the 1980s.

The absorbing atmosphere stoked our ambition levels, and we began to joke about whether we could be the instigators of a Mexican wave. Tactics came up. When should we attempt to start a wave - after a goal or during a lull? How would we convince thousands of people to join? Why would anyone listen to us? Did we have the courage? Would we survive the embarrassment?

We talked until kick-off, but inspiration eluded us. The clock ticked to 20 minutes, and aside from the guy in front secretly picking his nose, there was nothing to report. We had a sell-out crowd but with 31,000 subdued fans. It was an ideal time to make the magic happen, so we bit the bullet and reached out to the people around us, enthusing that when the clock reached 25 minutes, we'd collectively stand up and wave our arms around to start a Mexican wave. Our sales pitch met uninterested looks, polite smiles and vicarious embarrassment. On its face, the crowd didn't share our vision.

We waited anxiously as the minutes ticked by, hoping we'd got through to enough people to make it work. When the clock hit 25, there was nothing. Not even a fart. Metaphorical tumbleweeds blew through the stand. Moving into the 26th minute, not one person had bothered to scratch their arse, let alone throw their arms up in the air. Heck, we hadn't even stood up ourselves, so what chance was there if we hadn't got behind our own idea?

Despite our futile efforts, England did manage to score a goal through Steven Gerrard, which briefly lifted the crowd's spirits. Then, just as the referee was about to blow for half-time, Serbia and Montenegro managed an equaliser against the run of play, sending the crowd and the atmosphere back a notch. When the referee blew his whistle, we dashed to the toilets before our bladders exploded. Neither of us had wanted to urinate during the first half for fear that we might miss the birth of a Mexican wave.

As we demolished half-time steak pies, we agreed that we still had a chance of conceiving it. We also decided that a more hands-on approach was needed and that if people weren't going to listen to us, we had to make them.

Our new plan involved turning to the crowd at an agreed moment and yelling "MEXICAN WAVE" while pumping our arms up and down in the air. It was a direct approach, no doubt about it, and implementing it would not come to us naturally. The idea needed big cojones, even for Mad Ash, who considers public humiliation a close and personal friend.

We took our seats for the second half, and as we watched the clock tick by, we knew that we'd risk losing the momentum if we didn't act soon. It was getting close to the 60-minute mark when we looked at each other and agreed it was time. It was time for self-abasement. We took deep breaths, stood up, turned to the crowd, and began to yell,

"C'MON... MEXICAN WAVE... C'MON EVERY-BODY... LET'S START A MEXICAN WAVE... DON'T BE SCARED... IT'LL BE FUN!"

Our arms went up and down in mock messiah worship, flapping like fat turkeys that would never see the sky. My eyes focused on no one in particular, and to be honest, I was trying desperately to avoid eye contact with anyone. As my face began to turn red, I had an out of body experience looking at us from 20 rows back. If they'd thrown fruit, I'd have accepted it without question. We managed about 15 seconds of utter discomfort before Mad Ash motioned towards a bit of movement to our right. It was more of a Mexican ripple, but it was movement nonetheless.

We stared in disbelief as the motion rounded the corner flag and made its way along the stand opposite, picking up momentum at the same rate as my exhilaration. As it completed its first full lap, we leapt off our seats like the most devout worshippers, flinging our arms into the air as though we were somehow doubling its efforts. By now, it was a full-on, no holds barred, Mexican wave. I felt a small tear form in the corner of my eye. We'd done it.

Strangers looked over, pointing and smiling at the two clowns who hadn't given up hope. They'd seen our first attempt fail miserably, and now they witnessed our joy as we basked in the wave's glory. We shook hands and watched with pride as it circled the ground five or six times before petering out.

On top of the wave's success, England went on to win the game with a late Joe Cole goal, so it was mission accomplished on both fronts.

Viva Mexico.

The Final Peace

Peter Burns, London, UK

FOR CONTEXT, JEFF BECK WAS one of the 'big three' guitarists who'd been in 'The Yardbirds' rock band back in the 1960s. There was Eric Clapton, Jimmy Page and Jeff Beck, in that order.

I can't say I was enamoured with him around that time, but then, years later, in 1979, I was perusing Melody Maker album reviews and noticed one about Jeff. My gaze rested on 'glassy eyed', a comment from the reviewer describing his spellbound state after listening to the final track on side two of the vinyl disc. The track was called *'The Final Peace'*.

Of course, these were pre-Internet days, and for any new album, there was only one way to listen to it – buy the album. But it was Jeff Beck, and I'd never been a fan, so it was a significant outlay for something I might not like. My local record shop, Earthshaker, came to the rescue, which had the novel idea of running a library system for 50p a week (and the tacit understanding that you might, just might, tape it). But, if you really liked it, and might even want to *possess* it, 50p off the total price.

I got home with no great expectations. The cover was a plain black background with white writing and no photos, and sliding the pristine black vinyl LP out of the sleeve was always a tactile delight. It was more with curiosity than expectancy as I bent down to get eye-level with the spinning turntable deck and gently, ever so gently, released the last millimetres of the tonearm. Then it was touchdown of the diamond needle into the grooveless taxiing zone and take-off of the last track, '*The Final Peace*'. I could hear no lift-off. I even looked for the volume knob, as it was barely audible. I soon realised that it was a gently rising intro of repeated piano-like ostinato. Then, instantly, as the guitar entered, it soared up into an ever-rising celestial rhapsody.

'Glassy-eyed' is an understatement – the music is deeply emotional and moving, a serene hymn to deepest inner feelings.

Fast forward a few plays, and I have become obsessed with it. I glut on it. It takes me over. I have to stop listening to it. It's too strong. It reduces me to an overwhelmed state not conducive to everyday functioning. It can't just be listened to casually. It has to be prepared for. It has to be rationed. To listen to it casually is a sin.

We move on five years, and I'm with some mates in the bar of my local pub, the Half Moon in Putney, ready for a folk guitarist gig in the music room. I turn towards the bar, and he's there… Jeff Beck is there. In my local pub, with a small group of people, his friends, acolytes, who knows what they are. They see me looking over and nudging my mates, and I can read their supercilious expressions of 'keep your distance'.

Now I can empathise with this star-struck thing - I'm a teacher! I've experienced the star-struck bewilderment of six-year-olds seeing me off-stage, followed by their Monday morning, 'I saw you shopping' amazement at my other life.

My mind flashes to my mate's Tommy Cooper story, set in a Chiswick pub car park. When John sees *anybody* famous, he's straight in, gotta-talk-to-em. Approaching Tommy Cooper as he gets out of his car - no, he didn't have his Fez on – John comes out with an original, mind-blowing statement: 'You're Tommy Cooper!' Cooper tells him, 'Yeah… piss off!' and is gone without even a glance. But that was Tommy Cooper, and this is different. This is obsession.

Teetering forward, straining on the handbrake, my emotional clutch on the bite, my mate Mick tells me, 'Oh, no, you're not going to talk to him,' half-pleadingly out of who knows what – cringe-worthy embarrassment for me, and for being associated with me. However, his words are enough to sway me, so I settle back into the safety and calm of 'never-meet-your-idol'. I agree to move into the gig with my mates, so we pick up our glasses and move towards the music room.

And then, as the doorman starts to take our tickets, the obsession takes over. I peel away from the turning heads of my mates, past the raised eyebrows of his circle, and then suddenly, I am face to face with the man himself, Jeff Beck.

'I just want to thank you for that wonderful piece, *'The Final Peace'*… it's so beautiful,' I manage to get out. And as the group hushes into an embarrassed silence, Jeff smiles and sees, I think, that I'm smitten with the *piece* and not with him.

'Oh, thanks,' he nods gratefully towards me, as his *just-cos-I'm-famous* fears drop away. 'You know we just got it by chance. Tony Hymas played a few chords on the keyboard, and I started playing over the top, and it sounded quite special, so we decided to stop and not touch it until we got into the studio. We did it in just one take'.

'Well, I'm glad you did because I just love it. It's so moving. Thanks,' I tell him, and I start to move away.

'Thank you. Thanks for telling me.'

That was it – no less, no more.

And I still listen to *The Final Peace* in special moments.

Grooverider Featuring MC Stink

Lee Henaghan, Nelson, New Zealand

HAVING A CRAP IN MY idol Grooverider's toilet is the coolest thing I have ever done, which says quite a lot about me.

In February 2003, I'd been asked to interview the 'Rider' about his upcoming album and monthly club night at The End in London. It was my first cover story for Knowledge magazine, so I was already pretty damn pleased about it, but when I found out I was going to the bloke's house to do the interview, I got star-struck. You see, I'd worshipped the guy since I was a kid. The man is a drum & bass legend.

It wasn't the multi-million-pound mansion I thought it might be, but the place was plush enough. He had a fat BMW in the driveway, a television bigger than my bed and a badass stereo system. I dived straight into the interview, and everything was looking rosy, but after 10 minutes, I got the sudden urge for an almighty dump. This was encroaching massively on my quality idol time, so when his mobile phone went off, I used it as an ideal opportunity to nip upstairs and use the little boy's room.

So there I was, dropping a massive load in his swanked out bathroom, when it suddenly dawned on me that however old and senile I got, I would never, ever forget that moment—sitting on the john with my pants around my ankles, grinning like a loon and stinking out the bathroom of my musical hero.

Luckily he had one of those air fresheners on the wall where you have to press it once, so I covered my tracks by pressing it about five times before jogging back downstairs to finish the interview.

When my life flashes before my eyes, while I'm thinking about my children being born, graduating from university and marrying my wife, I'll also be thinking about Grooverider's toilet.

WORK ADVENTURERS

It's Official; Strawberries Send You Crazy
Domino Castor, Derry, Northern Ireland

ALTHOUGH IT DOESN'T SOUND BAD, picking strawberries for a living was truly demoralising. I've heard people say that it's character-building work, and it's not difficult to understand why. It breaks your back, wrecks your fingers, makes the most menial of tasks seem envious, and if you're incredibly unlucky, you'll get bitten by a spider! Still, if you enjoy working outside, getting a tan, meeting interesting characters, or sneaking the odd berry into your mouth, this might be the career for you.

Every backpacker I met who'd endured strawberry torture had a tale to tell. I remember Glenn, a British guy who'd quit during his first afternoon. As he walked away from the field, he turned to his rows of co-workers and shouted,

"YOU'RE MAD... ALL OF YOU... MAD I TELL YOU... WHY ARE YOU DOING THIS?... YOU HAVE A CHOICE... YOU DON'T HAVE TO DO THIS... YOU'VE GOT ROCKS IN YOUR HEADS... ALL OF YOU... AHH, FORGET IT... I'M OFF!"

At the hostel we stayed in, somebody had written a message about those little red devils on the back of a toilet door. Available for all those who sat on the John, it said:

"To anyone who is considering picking strawberries, STOP! STOP NOW! Ring your parents, use your credit card, steal the money if you need to, just DON'T allow yourself to go through the <u>HELL</u> of picking damn strawberries! Of course, some of you will choose to ignore this advice, so if you do, and subsequently work (or be a slave) at Twist's Farm, then please do us all a favour... punch Brad!"

THE BERRY TEAM

Ezmerelda's Calling

Keeley Topping, Vivo en Los Gallardos, Spain

I NEVER THOUGHT I'D HAVE to resort to picking fruit to fund my trip around Australia, and I think all first-time pickers make that mistake.

Before setting off Down Under, I'd vowed to do at least one day of it to see if all the horror stories were true. But when I arrived in Queensland and discovered that the only other career choice was deep-sea fishing, well, for an aqua-phobic woman like me, there weren't too many options, so it was either pick strawberries or starve!

Luckily I arrived at the end of May, which started the strawberry season and meant I'd spend my first week in the relative luxury of weeding the strawberry plants. This part of the job basically 'allowed' us to kneel in front of the strawberry plants and pick out the weeds, spiders and dead frogs. Only later did I realise what a treat this was in comparison!

I quickly learned that the basics of strawberry picking were as follows:

- You bent over at a 90-degree angle to pick each ripe strawberry in each row until you filled your tray or until your back broke, whichever came first.
- When your tray was full, you took it to the truck, got a new one, and started all over again, without taking a break, and in my case, without straightening my back. This continued for eight hours a day, six days a week.

Also, please bear in mind the following:

- You had to use both of your hands and couldn't even lean on one of them. As my boss, Mr Grizzly, would grumble, "You were given two hands, weren't you? WELL, USE THEM!" He was an arsehole.
- They covered the strawberries in a pesticide that caused the skin on your hands to flake away, and this left you looking like you had a skin problem.
- You weren't supposed to talk to your co-workers.
- You weren't allowed to kneel.
- You should never drop strawberries into the tray. "STOP BRUISING MY FRUIT!" Mr Grizzly again.
- Most importantly, you were never, ever to lean on your tray. It was a sackable offence, I'll have you know!
- Add in a 10 minute morning break, plus 20 minutes for lunch, and you're starting to understand the life of a strawberry picker.

And now that I've destroyed the fruit picking industry for you let me point out a couple of its positive aspects. Australia's glorious sun shone constantly, so we got incredible tans and looked healthier than we ever had before - back at the hostel in the evenings, it was pretty obvious who'd been working in the fields! Then there were the team members who picked year in and year out. They were some of the weirdest and wildest characters you could ever meet. I'll never forget an age-old Vietnamese woman called Toy who'd been picking strawberries since the year before I was born, whereas at least I only had to save enough to move to Cairns!

A day of this back-breaking monotony made me a grand total of $104, so considering my only outgoings were rent, noodles and boxed wine, I was able to build a nest egg reasonably quickly. And for that much, I was grateful because it only took four weeks before the strawberries broke me, and I had to take early retirement.

Twelve months later, I was thankful that I could finally stand up straight again, and my hands no longer resembled a leper's. Please spare a thought for my friends who stuck the job out for six months, though - they're now all appearing in various stage productions of the Hunchback of Notre Dame.

Canadian Shark Bait

Mark Oleniuk, Saskatoon, Saskatchewan, Canada

LIKE MOST BACKPACKERS, DURING MY time in Australia, I ran short of money and had to find alternative funding to keep my dream alive. If I wasn't going to rob a bank, this could only mean one thing - I had to find work.

After a few days of picking strawberries and realising that the shitty pay wasn't worth the backbreaking monotony, I decided to look elsewhere. Be warned; fruit picking is truly horrendous, the worst job I ever had, so don't even go there. The memories still send a shiver down my spine, literally.

I lived near a fishing community at the time, so I took a walk down to the docks one morning and asked a few shady characters if they were hiring. I'd heard from a fellow traveller that there was good money to be made as a commercial fisherman, so I filled out an application form, left it with a shifty looking captain and let my mind dream up a few deep-sea adventures.

Being a prairie kid from Canada, I live about as far from the ocean as possible, so an opportunity like this was rare. Giant squids and treasure maps, pirate ships and mermaids would be something to tell the folks about back home, not to mention a great story for my grandkids, if I survived. A few days later, a phone call told me to pack a bag and be at the docks early the following day. We were setting sail, and I had a new job as a deckhand.

Living and working on a boat for upwards of 10 days at a time threw up plenty of highs and lows, with throwing up being one of the lows. I experienced things I would never have back home, and a great example of this would be the scary incident I had with a very large and aggressive fish.

It was my second tour of duty on a blisteringly hot day with a dead calm sea and fish that weren't biting much. After pulling in some rudderfish that weren't too profitable on the fish market, early in the afternoon, we got a bite, and it looked big. We began to pull in our catch and what we found on the end of the line was an angry 10-foot Mako shark thrashing about as if its life depended on it, which it did. It reminded me of an out of control fire hose, and the strength it displayed was frightening.

The standard procedure was to get a shark noose around its neck, tighten it and then pull the shark on board to claim our catch. One of my crew-mates got the Mako up close to the boat, and my job was to get the noose around it; not a pleasant job, I know, but I needed to earn some coin and sure as hell didn't want to pick another strawberry.

The noose was essentially a piece of cable with a clip on one end and a rope on the other, attached to a large diesel reservoir on deck. I managed to get the noose positioned around the Mako's neck, tugged at it and no sooner had I done this than the shark took off, fast. Usually, this wouldn't be a problem as the large diesel tank is so heavy that even a great white couldn't shift it, but for some reason, the last person who used it hadn't secured the clip.

So with our prize catch swimming away, all I had was slack rope flying through my grip until the clip hit my hands and dug in, which is not a good thing when you have an angry 300lb fish on the end. Even with blood seeping from my hands, I couldn't let go of the rope and clip, or I'd be in big trouble. Fishermen's stories involve fearlessness, meanness, and death and often contain immense pain, terrible discomfort and again death, so bloody hands would not be enough of an excuse for losing the fish. I had no choice but to hold on.

As I fought with the shark, my attention shifted from pulling it on board to preventing my ass from falling overboard into the shark-infested waters. Falling into the ocean wearing your Wellington boots is wildly hazardous and certainly doesn't help prevent yourself from drowning or swimming away from sharks, either. As I held the rope with one hand and the railing of the boat with the other, the skipper screamed out,

"You better not lose that fish, boy… if you lose that fish, you're gonna lose your life!"

Earlier in the trip, the skipper had told me that he'd been a fisherman his whole life, which led to questions about the life of a fisherman. Of the resulting answers, there was one in particular that worried me and, for some reason, popped into my head at that exact point: *'Nobody can hear you scream at sea.'*

It got me thinking that if I lost the shark, then I was probably going overboard, which was wildly irrational but at the time seemed perfectly feasible. I was getting to the point where I'd have happily traded positions with a strawberry picker, and that's saying something! I was straight-up scared, which fishermen rarely are, yet something I wasn't afraid to admit. As I strained every sinew of my body to keep hold of that damned rope, each second felt like a minute.

Finally, after what felt like forever, my crew-mates assembled, pulled me back from the edge of the boat, and we began to haul the shark in. 30 minutes of fight later, and with my hands a bloody raw mess, we finally landed that Mako, and he was magnificent.

I thoroughly enjoyed most of my time working on the boats, but I'd have to say that the shark experience was probably the most frightening of my entire life.

Now I see why most people don't want the job.

Steamy Windows On The Motorway

Heidi Humphrey, Swindon and Wiltshire's
GWR FM, UK

IT'S PRETTY ALARMING THAT I used to get paid to talk rubbish for a living. Granted, the word 'rubbish' wasn't used in my job description, but being a breakfast radio presenter did take pub gossiping to a whole new level. Rather than sitting in the Dog and Duck telling three friends about my hilarious weekend or putting down a hated celebrity after their latest outburst, I got to share it with thousands of listeners instead.

Admittedly, getting up at 4.30 am was a pain in the arse, but every job has its price and starting that early meant I was always home by lunchtime to watch my favourite Australian soap. Plus, when summertime arrived, I had endless amounts of lazy afternoons to work on a tan that never seemed to fade.

With our shows being live and unpredictable, the listeners often helped guide our success, and you'd be shocked by the amount of hair-raising content we'd sift through that couldn't be aired. Our audience did some weird things over their weekends!

Simply touching on how my boyfriend had relieved himself into my sock drawer on a Saturday night helped turn a tap that gushed with housewives calling in. A joke in passing could easily create a forum for ladies desperate to talk about their husband's drunken sleepwalking or wee habits, meaning the masses often magnified my escapades.

Various perks came with the job, and using a little subtlety meant I could often get my hands on a few things I wanted, plus the odd few bits I genuinely needed. All I had to do was mention in passing that I had a leaky tap, and before I knew it, six plumbers were calling to say they'd fix it for free. And if I talked about a commercial I'd seen for a new movie, there'd be free cinema tickets or DVDs sitting on the doormat within a week.

Occasionally, I was presented with an opportunity to interview mainstream bands and singers. At times, they'd invite me to an exclusive gig for a glass or two of champagne in the hope of a smidgeon of positive publicity. These gigs left me with the fondest of memories, mainly because of the intimacy of the venues they'd play.

From time to time, I'd also attend public events where I'd cut ribbons or have a few drinks in a newly opened bar or nightclub. I found this quite ironic because I worked on the radio, so it wasn't as if the public knew my face. Still, I wasn't complaining and was always grateful to be asked, and once people knew what I did for a living, I'd often get the old VIP treatment.

Over the years, I've been asked many questions about working on the radio. One question crops up more than any other, though - what was my funniest ever moment on a live show?

Well, that's easy. It was the day a random listener called in to tell us that she'd just seen a couple having a bit of nooky in the back of a car. It was parked on the lay-by of a busy dual carriageway in Swindon at 7.30 am, and the poor lady was taking her kids to school. The sighting was quickly confirmed by an orderly queue of nosy motorists calling in, and even our travel plane spotted it. The couple mustn't have been listening to us, though, as they inadvertently helped us have our most memorable show. Listeners called in their droves, describing the bare bobbing arse they spotted through the steamy windows!

Putting it simply, presenting on the radio was a dream for me, and it was more like having fun than going to work. I'm a damn lucky person to have had the opportunity.

ALTRUISTIC ADVENTURERS

Retail, African Style
Tim Scott, Birmingham, UK

I STOOD IN THE DOORWAY of my new home, watching an infant wave a burning torch just inches from his grandmother's highly flammable house. I'd been in Zambia for three days, having quit my job in London to see a little more of the world - I just hadn't banked on that world being sent up in flames by a devil child!

As I moved to snatch the flame from his grasp, I heard his sister scream and then freeze. I couldn't stop a smile creeping across my face as her scream turned to laughter. Rather than choosing which child to save first, I joined in the riotous giggling that filled the air like smoke. As it transpired, the children were yelling, "SNAKE!" and then collapsing into fits of hysteria.

What I'd taken to be a bad situation was simply a game. The kids in the village took any opportunity to do dangerous things with fire. One day it would be snakes; the next it would be ants as they waved the fire around until they thought the 'threat' had gone or until they became tired, whichever came first. I let the experts continue; they seemed to know what they were doing.

The following morning, grandma's house was unmarked, and the devils of the previous evening were marching to school; no fire this time, just wide contagious grins as they passed. I surveyed the scene. Here I was, miles from anywhere, young, in love, and content. And I had no idea what I was meant to be doing. I'd come to Africa to work in a community for a few months while my girlfriend Anna taught history and English. The community needed a shop to support its educational programmes, and I was the man chosen to build and stock it. All I knew was that I was standing in a lemon grove, feeling slightly dishevelled and wondering where the inspiration I'd need would come from.

You don't have to be a genius to know that Zambia has had a hard time. In the 1960s, it was wealthy and optimistic, then the economy collapsed, and things have been steadily getting worse. I bowled up, thinking that I could make a big difference to the community, but I quickly realised that it would be I who'd gain the most from my visit.

The Great North Road is a ribbon of tarmac that seems to run the country's length. Unlike most Zambians, I saw an awful lot of it. Every week or so, I'd travel to a local town at least two hours away to plan the delivery of supplies - well, in theory, at least. What happened, in reality, was that I'd get pulled from pillar to post by the more creative members of my team who had their own agendas, and I'd have to fight pretty hard to forward my own 'programme'. Everyone seemingly used the p-word, and I was powerless to resist picking it up.

Those trips were nothing if not original. I was hypnotised by the road, the sense of movement, the sun and the sounds. We always met for our research trips by the office in the village, set up by one of Anna's relatives in the early 1990s. The marker always propped up against the same tree, a lurid pink bicycle. When we arrived home tired, dirty, and happy, it was our guiding light.

We'd usually get as many people as possible into whatever vehicle was available on a typical trip. My favourite memory was of *seventeen* of us squeezed into an antique Land Rover, accompanied by a very feisty pig in a bag! On that trip, I shared a front seat with two others but had to hang out of the window as it was so cramped. It offered me a view of the back wheel, and that view wasn't good.

"John!" I yelled, roughly in the direction of where I thought the driver would be sitting, though, with so many bodies, it was a bit of a guess.

"John, stop the truck... stop it IMMEDIATELY!"

We pulled over to the side of the road, and 17 people and a pig hopped out. I showed them that a back wheel was only being held in place by one bolt rather than the usual six, and that bolt was about to come loose! Nobody panicked or got angry, nuts and bolts were cannibalised from other wheels, and we were soon on our way again. What would have happened if it had dropped off and we'd flipped over? I couldn't help but wonder. Despite our oblivious dangers, we returned each time safely.

These journeys were always filled with unusual sounds and an expanded sense of space. I became accustomed to huddling against the back of a pickup as we hurtled into the darkness and sat on either an oily tank of gas or a rickety church bench. I grew fond of stopping at the side of the road to smoke a cigarette in the chill evening air, still miles from home. The driver could deliver what the others wanted, a moment of space and time to reflect on being nothing more than men away from the village.

The penultimate trip was perhaps my most extraordinary. Have you ever looked at a night sky through weakened headlights? The world shrinks, and your imagination conjures all kinds of unexpected images. We'd made yet another stop, even though it was late and most of us wanted to get back to the village. What frightened me that night wasn't a vast fire close by but the sight of a creature that looked like it had been in hibernation for several millennia. It swooped low, spanning half the track, and in an instant banked hard right, cutting through the trees. Though it was illuminated for only a few seconds, its leathery wings made a definitive clap in my mind, and its tusk-like beak will forever be etched onto the back of my eyes. Pterodactyl is perhaps an exaggeration, but it was more Spielberg-esque than anything I'm used to. To this day, I have no idea what it was.

I came to learn that the bush is full of people. Communities thrive in happiness, belief, drunkenness, commerce, humour and hope. Stand still for a moment, and you'll find company. My village was full of sounds that seemed clearer in the prevailing quiet. The splutter of an engine, the school bell, a battered transistor radio, the scratching in spiky leaves of ugly haggard hens, hymns and prayers, the wind and the sound of footsteps; they were all present. Reverence for sounds rather than music was a welcome relief.

We drink to forget, laugh to make friends, and somehow I felt more like myself than usual. Like the children I passed in the tiny crèche next to my 'office', I skipped everywhere. Thatchers and craftsmen came and went, a market was held, and plans were drawn. The shop got there, but I'm not sure it changed the community. The community just continued. Burning brightly.

I look fondly upon the mark it left on me.

Peace Amongst Chaos

Paras Purohit, London, UK

"CHAI! CHAI! CHAI! CHAI! CHAI!"

The saying goes that the streets of Calcutta never sleep, but it always amazed me just how full of life they were at 5.30 am. Chai stalls buzzed with activity as their vendors hustled for business, telling anyone within 100 metres to buy their small clay urns of tea.

My nostrils awoke with the smells of vegetable curries and puris being cooked. Though I never had curry for breakfast back home in London, my stomach governed thought in India, and temptation usually won. As I squelched through the sticky mud on crowded lanes, I imagined mouth-watering foods sliding down into my noisy stomach. Even though I'd walked that same zany route every day for a month, it never failed to move me.

Knock, knock. No answer. I arrived at a locked door at Mother Theresa House, but the hymns hadn't started, so I decided to ring the bell and plead innocence. As if it was a sign, the opening verse of *Morning Has Broken* rose above the din of the street, and I resigned myself to sitting there for an hour until mass had finished.

I slumped in the doorway and closed my eyes, disappointed at being late for my final morning but grateful for the rest it offered. Moments later, the door opened, and the familiar face of Sister Karina smiled down upon me. After telling her I'd be attending mass that morning, she'd kept her eye out for me, so I thanked her and made my way up the stairs and into the chapel expecting disapproving looks. All I received from the Sisters and my fellow volunteers were radiant smiles.

Mother Theresa House is situated on AJC Bose Road in the heart of Calcutta and is home to The Missionaries of Charity, the order of nuns founded by Mother herself. Like most others in Calcutta, AJC Bose Road is never dull, quiet, or empty, and even at 6 am, truck horns blared, and frantic traffic provided a constant hum. No matter how loud things were on the exterior, nothing could pierce the serenity inside the chapel.

After the service, we made our way downstairs to where the Sisters had laid out cups of chai and a selection of fruit. The volunteers politely collected their portions and gathered in the courtyard, where the sun offered warmth. I wanted to pay one last visit to Mother Theresa's grave, so I walked past the volunteers and politely rejected their offers to sit with them. At the far end of the courtyard, I entered Mother's tomb and final resting place, a large simple room with a rectangular concrete block in the centre.

"Mother's" – I spoke of her as familiarly as the Sisters.

Many people had already gathered around her grave, some standing, others kneeling or lying face down, but all were praying. I stood at the back so as not to disturb anyone, and my eyes went straight to the inscription on her tomb, a passage from The Bible. The book and chapter elude me, but it said, "*Love one another, as I have loved you.*" I couldn't think of an epitaph more appropriate; it was short, simple and perfect.

The time had come to make the final journey to my workplace, Prem Dan, and as I left the convent, I passed a few beggars outside who raised themselves to ask for spare rupees. It was uncomfortable to see fellow volunteers ignore them, despite seeing those same volunteers help others less fortunate. I guess it's easy to be kind and caring when everybody else is, but also thick-skinned and dismissive when it suits. Conformity is one of the more deeply rooted human traits, and they were on their own journey of discovery.

In Hindi, 'Prem' means love, and 'Dan' means a charitable donation or gift, so Prem Dan essentially means The Gift of Love. Like Mother's inscription on her tomb, I felt this was an apt summary. Prem Dan is one of seven centres in Calcutta run by The Missionaries of Charity to provide care for the long-term sick, especially the mentally disabled. They operate many more worldwide and act as emergency centres for people who require urgent medical treatment without the means to afford it. The majority of Calcutta's population is poor, so the volume of patients across the centres is high.

At the bus stop, scores of volunteers wait in the chaos that sweeps Indian cities daily. Crazed conductors jump from slowing buses to scream destinations at the hoards. On seeing the volunteers, they enthusiastically shout the names of the centres.

"KALIGHAT!" "SHANTI DAN!" "SHISHU BHA-VAN!" "PREM DAN... PREM DAN!"

Our bus, number 202, careened up the packed street, testing people's reflexes to get out of its way. Our driver had one hand on the steering wheel and the other on the horn as he screeched to a halt, allowing our group to rush forward as one and squeeze on. In record time, the conductor had ushered the hapless but kind-willed westerners onto the overcrowded death machine. I let everyone on before me, and when there was no room left, I jumped onto the back as it pulled away, Bollywood-style. I clung on for dear life with an unhinged bus conductor hanging next to me.

The journey took half an hour, and I was always fascinated by the stark contrast of urban areas as we hurtled through Calcutta. There were areas of such wealth that houses wouldn't look out of place in Park Lane or Mayfair, yet they were situated next to shacks of such poverty that you wouldn't think the human spirit could cope. But cope, it did. And in places, it thrived.

Upon reaching Bridge Number Four, we got the best view of the surrounding slums that stretched out in all directions without forgiveness. We could read the massive sign saying 'PREM DAN', a beacon of hope in a quagmire of decay.

Like lemmings, we jumped from the bus while it still moved. This always struck me as odd because why did buses never have enough time to stop for a country that worked as painfully slowly as India did? Nevertheless, I took stock of my surroundings and saw that life was abundant in Calcutta. Women sat outside houses gossiping and peeling vegetables, men stood talking to one another or working, and a few older children flew kites. I couldn't think of anything more symbolic than the act of flying a kite in the slum. People's hopes soaring high above their appalling standing in life.

As we made our way through the tiny streets and gullies, a ragtag gang of street children accosted us shouting the only three English words they knew, "HELLO! MONEY! CHOCOLATE!" A few of us stopped to play, picking them up and swinging them high over our heads as they screamed with laughter.

Again, I was surprised to see a few Prem Dan volunteers walk past these desperate kids without giving them the time of day. I wondered if this could have been aversion therapy, like the first time you see something scary, it scares you, but once you've seen it ten times, it scares you less. Then, after you see it 100 times, it becomes passé. At the beginning of their time at Prem Dan, did these volunteers stop for the kids? Being relatively fresh to the environment, seeing them still moved me. But if I stayed for a year or even ten years, would I ignore them too?

We knocked on Prem Dan's gate, and a doorman slid the shutter across to see who it was. The Missionaries must have thought that this holy place, which is in the middle of chaos, wouldn't survive without locked gates, and that to me seemed almost a contradiction in terms.

Prem Dan is a large facility containing 200 people where men and women are strictly segregated into opposite buildings with a common area in the middle. No female volunteers are allowed into the male section and vice versa. In the men's section, there are two large wards for patients, and both lead out to a covered porch with chairs and beds where the patients relax during the day.

Upon arrival, other volunteers had already moved the patients outside. Our first job of the day was to clean the wards. When I started three weeks back, this seemed like the most burdensome task. Some of the patients had no control over their bodily functions, and it gave the air a stomach-churning odour. On a damp Calcutta morning, the oppressive humidity and powerful aromas could be quite the baptism of fire!

We started by sweeping the floors with straw brooms. Because of their design, the small hand brooms meant we had to get a lot closer to the stench than we'd have liked, but as they were the only ones available, we got on with it. It was a most unpleasant task as we poured water around the rooms, scrubbed the floors with soap, rinsed with more water and then swept the excess through the doors. After the wards were clean, the patients were moved back inside, and we repeated the process on the porch.

Next up that morning, I helped shave an elderly man with no teeth and Turret's syndrome while his peers sat around teasing him. When I say there was a nonstop outburst of violent expletives from him, it's not an exaggeration. And due to his jerky movements, I was constantly worried that I would cut him at any moment. Thankfully though, both he and I got through it unscathed.

Then it was onto the main event, assisting John, an Irish builder who'd unexpectedly found himself as the Head Surgeon of Prem Dan. He was a tough character with strong morals and the trademark Irish sense of humour. We discussed the latest in-patients with a group of other first-aid volunteers; it was a custom mix of building site mishaps, traffic accidents, and TB sufferers. We prioritised them as best we could and got to work, John treating the patients while I retrieved medical supplies, passed him instruments and applied uncomplicated dressings. A long line of patients filtered down the walkway waiting patiently for the courageous, untrained volunteers to attend them.

First up was Cookie, a skinny boy of 14 years old with the broadest and most unsymmetrical smile I'd ever seen; its sheer breadth and crookedness accentuated its perfection. He'd been caught stealing rice, and he'd fallen and cut his shin to the bone during his escape. However, with no money for treatment, the wound became infected over the following days. Now he was sitting in front of us with his leg in a bucket of disinfectant. I put on a pair of surgical gloves and silently winced when I looked at the wound before picking the maggots from it, both dead and alive. There were moments when I thought he'd scream, simply because I would have, but all he did was wince sharply before grinning and motioning for us to continue. Incredibly, he was still smiling when we finished dressing it.

Next up was a mentally disabled man with a weeping hip sore no bigger than a coin. As we punctured the wound and squeezed the reeking puss from it, he screamed as though we were sawing his legs off. I couldn't bear to look at him, and every time he screamed, it killed a piece of me inside. When we finished, he was no different, and there were no thanks, just the same lifeless expression as before. What had I been expecting?

For my last case at Prem Dan, we treated a rickshaw driver who had lost half of his foot in a motor accident, something that's all too common in India. He still had his big toe and the next one along, but then his foot was sliced off in a straight line almost to his ankle. Small pieces of white bone protruded from his pink flesh, giving it the look of a well-used comb missing a few teeth. Similarly to Cookie, he'd been sitting patiently with his foot in a bucket of disinfectant, so I helped him to the table and set about the most unpleasant job of cleaning and dressing it. I could only imagine the pain he was going through as we picked away the dirt and poured disinfectant directly onto it, yet he didn't flinch once. Not once. As he sat there holding up the mangled foot, he looked at the injury and us with a detached interest. I was in awe of his pain threshold and couldn't help comparing him to the disabled man with the tiny wound, realising my mistake immediately.

Having finished our cases for the morning, it was time for lunch's daily military operation. Several volunteers carried enormous curry pots, rice and dhal to the walkway, placing them on tables piled high with plates. The patients had already begun queuing for food, even though they were aware of the golden rule that we always fed those less able first. It was only after we'd taken care of those patients that we served any food, and I loved how they coordinated this.

Serving often involved turning down daily requests for, "Just a *little* more, *please*, uncle." It was difficult saying no, but we had no choice as there wasn't enough for second helpings. The clean-up operation began when we served the last plate, just like a giant chain. Four volunteers washed dishes while the others cleaned the porch and walkway, now splattered with food. I usually washed dishes, but today, with permission, I snuck off to say goodbye to a few of my favourite patients.

I found the kids playing together in their usual spot under the trees, so I handed out the biscuits I'd brought, and they stuffed them into their mouths. The kids were delirious with excitement, running and jumping all around me. They didn't seem to listen when I said I was leaving Prem Dan, but they wanted to follow as I made one last lap of the compound.

Naresh, a young man with acute cerebral palsy who couldn't walk or speak properly, hailed me with his usual, "Hello uncle... carry, uncle, carry!" I never could resist, so I carried him for one lap of Prem Dan as he chatted with the children. When we returned to our starting point, he repeated, "Carry, uncle, carry!" I smiled and put him down, telling him I was too tired for another lap. He said goodbye and immediately turned his attention to the next volunteer. I knew he'd forget me in a heartbeat.

Finally, it was time to leave. I said emotional goodbyes to the Sisters and walked away from this modern-day miracle with my head held high. As I took my last steps out of the front gate, I couldn't help turning my thoughts to tomorrow. Who would help John? Who would bring little gifts for the children? I wanted to think they'd remember me, but I wasn't sure. I wanted to believe that I'd made a difference, but as I walked back through the slum, I realised that it was the tiniest of drops in the largest of oceans.

In the slum, the children were still flying kites. When I'm older and have children, I'll teach them to fly kites. It's a good enterprise. A hopeful enterprise.

HEDONISTIC ADVENTURERS

House Party 1992

Robert Ahnston, San Franciso, US

I LIVED IN A HOUSE with four other people at the time, or at least I think it was four. It's hard to say because we had nine or ten different housemates at one point or another in 1992. At the peak of our popularity and desire to party, we'd thrown a massive party the previous semester. Still, we wanted to out-do ourselves by throwing the mother of all parties the second time around.

At the expense of the University Engineering Department (where I was in the work/study program), I made a bunch of flyers. After handing them out to all of our friends, my roommate Jason and I spent an hour a day handing them out in the busy West Mall area of the university in the few days leading up to it. We were expecting a big crowd, but what we got was ridiculous. It was totally out of control. Here's a quick rundown of the evening:

We got five kegs of beer at 5 pm.

By 6 pm, the house was already full.

At 7 pm, I remember looking over our balcony and see-ing a sea of people inside our privacy fence, reminiscent of the party in the movie Weird Science. A traffic jam had built up from the constant train of cars going by sounding their horns, to the obvious delight of our neighbours. The success of the last party had spread through word of mouth, carrying most of our friends (and their friends) to the house earlier than expected. At this point, I questioned whether handing out flyers on campus had been a good idea. I would ask myself that same question many more times over the following 24 hours.

By 8 pm, the Police Department and the Alcoholic Beverage Commission were standing at the front door. Luckily they didn't pull the plug on the party, but they did warn us not to let anyone walk outside with a drink in their hand. Those who lived there took shifts to help implement their orders for the rest of the night. What happened after 8 pm is a blur, but the aftermath included the following:

Someone did a keg stand on the front porch and fell through our living room window. We never did get this window repaired, and I remember it being chilly in that room for a long while afterwards.

Before the party, we had four or five electric razors in the house. After the party, we had none.

I did a stage dive off our stairwell, which caused someone to fall into a wall and create a two-foot hole. We never got this repaired.

When the fifth keg floated, my roommate Pat decided to spend what little money he had left on buying two more. After selling his car for $500 a few days earlier, he felt flush. Our initial costs were about $100 per roommate, so with Pat putting in another $150, he put half of his car into that party.

Sometime before midnight, a neighbour came in to complain about the noise. A month later, my roommate Jeremy and I would spend an afternoon in court defending ourselves. Luckily, we won the case. Nevertheless, Jeremy *was* arrested around midnight when the police learned that there was a warrant out for his arrest, which was something to do with outstanding traffic violations. I spent the next three hours trying to get him out of jail.

Several people spent the night with us, so I went on a taco run for breakfast early the following day. I came back to be greeted by five or six 'representatives' from the neighbourhood, shouting at me for throwing a crazy party and making a mess of the streets. To get back on their good side, I gathered everyone together, and we walked around picking up trash. I was taken aback to find that the partygoers had spread destruction for two blocks in each direction, with our house at its centre. There were beer bottles, burger wrappers, condoms, flyers, streamers, cigarette butts, homemade bongs, and weird substances stuck in places you couldn't imagine.

After this party, we toned down each one we threw after that, plus we rejected any ideas of ever handing out flyers again. It's funny when I think about it now, but it wasn't just a legendary night - it was also the first time I met four people who would become highly influential in my life, including my wife.

God bless college parties.

"You *cannot* wear those to the Mansion!"

Neil Hogan, UK and Ireland

"ARE YOU STILL HEADED TO Mexico this Friday?" Neil asked.

"Yes, that's the plan," I said.

"So you don't want to go to a party at the Playboy Mansion then?"

"What? Are you crazy? I'd give a kidney!"

"That's OK, I understand, you have plans, you can't make it, I understand. I'll ask someone else."

"Hang on a minute… Mexico can wait; it's not going anywhere!"

And that's how the phone call went. It was March 2008, and one minute I was travelling to Mexico; the next, I had an invite to the Playboy Mansion.

I met Neil Mandt in 2002 in Ho Chi Minh City, Vietnam. It was quite the introduction, with the night culminating in hot-jar massages as we lay semi-naked on the pavement of a busy downtown street. After a few nights of clowning around, talk turned to what we did for a living back home. It came to pass that he was a film director in Hollywood.

"Film director, yeah, right mate… I'm not that gullible!" It turned out he was a film director.

Neil is highly confident, assertive, and as loyal as they come. He's also a brilliant salesman who could sell sand in a desert, and an eternal adventurer with more than 100 countries under his belt, so his repertoire of funny stories is vast.

We maintained contact after Vietnam, and in 2004 he wanted to film a short travel story of an extract from this book, so he flew over to England with his production crew and unexpectedly asked me to act in the piece. The story became a small part of a comedy feature film he later released called *Last Stop for Paul*, which became the world's highest award-winning independent film of 2007, winning 45 awards globally. Subsequently, Neil invited me over to Los Angeles for the cinematic premiere, which brings us to the start of this story, the Playboy Mansion invitation.

So there I was, looking out over Laurel Canyon at a plush pad in the Hollywood Hills, having just accepted an invitation to the Playboy Mansion. If somebody had pulled my arm off and begun to beat me with it at that moment, I'd have thought nothing of it. After all, surely I was dreaming.

The Playboy Mansion is one of the most famous residences in Los Angeles, and its owner at the time, Hugh Hefner, had a reputation for throwing many historical parties. We were going to the party as a production crew for the sports network ESPN, but once the filming finished, we'd be putting the cameras away to enjoy the party. Head of the crew was Neil's brother, Michael, who's six-two and 215lbs, as they say in the States. I always talk sports with him and would say he's taught me more about baseball, basketball, and American football than anyone else, but then he was the Jim Rome sports show producer for 7 years.

"Hogan, have you got your pyjamas ready for the party on Saturday night?" he asked.

"Pyjamas?" I asked, confused. "*It's going to be a pyjama party!?*" My friends back home were going to love this.

While in Los Angeles, I had a funky little scooter that my buddy Ron Carlson had lent me. It looked like a cat but barked like a dog, and every day I rode it, I'd receive an abundance of fun comments, usually from people next to me at traffic lights. The day after the chat with Michael, I rode to four different clothes stores before I found anything pyjama related and even then, it was only a pair of bottoms. Safe in knowing that I wouldn't be turning up to the party naked, I bought a pair. Later that day, however, I was left scratching my head when Neil's cousin Larry said,

"Hey, numb-nuts, you should have shopped a bit more upmarket than Target for a party like this!"

I knew he was right but justified my purchase through the time allotted to the search. Besides, I wanted to see how many other cheapskates had also shopped at Target, and I'd be able to spot them easy enough now that I knew their entire line of three pairs. The pyjama escapade left me feeling there was a gap in the pyjama market in Hollywood, which considering the frequency of these parties, was quite surprising. To complete the outfit, I'd wear a white t-shirt with a long cream dressing gown to disguise my lack of a two-piece and general shabbiness.

On the night of the party, our rendezvous was the Roosevelt Hotel in Hollywood, so we headed over in Neil's Porsche, parked on Orange Drive and walked the rest of the way, much to the amusement of those we passed. When we reached Hollywood Boulevard, someone stopped us and said,

"Hey, *coooool* outfits, dude, where's the pyjama party?"

"The Playboy Mansion," Neil replied, sounding like he was a regular.

"Whoa... far out, man!" I looked for a surfboard but couldn't see one.

They had organised shuttles to take guests to the Mansion, and as we registered, I saw men dressed in colourful smoking jackets and silk pyjamas in the main (no cheap crap from Target).

The shuttle ride didn't take long, and at first glance, the Mansion looked like something out of a Hans Christian

Andersen fairy tale. The trees entwined with fairy lights, a huge fountain on the driveway, and lawns so manicured they'd make a golfer drool. As I got off the shuttle, I felt giddy.

The American footballer Akin Ayodele was hosting the piece for us. He was the linebacker for the Miami Dolphins and a big scary dude, especially if you looked up and saw him running at you full speed (six-two, 245 lbs). As we wandered through the party, we stopped to film him speaking with various sports stars, though as I was still learning my Andy Roddicks from my Drederick Tatums, I didn't recognise anyone.

After wrapping up the segment - the most pleasurable hour of work I have ever done - I put the camera in the cloakroom and poked my head into the famous grotto filled with umpteen scantily clad ladies. At the bar, I ordered margaritas all around, and as I handed over the money was told that it was a free bar.

The party's heart was inside a large outdoor marquee where guests danced, and food was laid out. Now that I had time to survey the scene, the ratio appeared to be about four women to every guy. There were Playboy Bunnies scattered throughout, and as the tent heated up, a few guests felt the need to lose what little they were wearing. I'd never seen anything quite like it in my life.

I chatted to a few girls, had a dance, got a drink and mingled with guests. Then I did it all over again and again. At one point, I pinched myself as I drank a beer with David Walliams and wondered if we were the only two Brits representing from back home.

I wandered and smiled, chatted and posed, gawped and burped, danced and pointed and laughed. The place was like no other, and the party was incomparable, especially for its surrealism.

The first time I went to Los Angeles in 2004, Neil got me involved with the ESPN sports awards show, the ESPYs, where I met plenty of familiar faces, and for someone from a small city, it felt like a once in a lifetime experience. I didn't think a second visit to LA could eclipse the first, but it did. All I can do is thank the guy. He gave me a glimpse into the world of Hollywood show business, and without him as a friend, I would never have had that opportunity. So cheers, mate, the memories will last a lifetime.

Oh, and to fill you in, I didn't see anyone wearing pyjamas from Target at the party. Larry was right; I should have shopped a bit more upmarket.

Champagne, Anyone?

Wolfgang Rohr, San Diego, US

STANDING IN TIMES SQUARE AS the clock turned to a New Year was something I'd aspired to since watching Dick Clark as a child. Growing older and watching the ball drop every midnight became a moment I equated with the quintessential New Year celebration.

I remember bragging to friends in high school that I'd do this someday in my future, and I'm sure I made it sound like it would be the greatest trip of all time. I'd find a little money, get away from the family for a few days, and fly to New York to live it out precisely as they did on TV. It was all talk at the time, but it stayed in my mind for a date I knew not when. It wasn't until 1998 that I decided to move that thought from the back of my mind to front and centre.

When I arrived in New York that December, it was cold. I know that seems obvious, but maybe I didn't stress it enough. It was *really* cold. It was balls into gut cold. It was nipples could cut ice cold. It was vapours from your breath icing in your eyes cold. I must have been wearing three layers of clothes, wrapped in a heavy coat and with all the accessories (scarf, hood, gloves), yet even with all of this on, when I turned a corner on Fifth Avenue and caught a gust of wind, it felt as though I was completely naked.

That day my friends and I conserved our energy, as we knew we'd be putting in a good shift on the streets. For those of you who aren't aware, if you want to stand in Times Square for the dawn of a New Year, you must stand there for a very long time. You can't just rock up at 11.30 pm and say, "Excellent, I made it in time… I'll just duck into this bar for a quick drink and stay out of the elements until it gets to countdown."

If it were that simple, the logistics would be too much for the city to handle. No, to perform this feat of endurance, you need to be out on the streets by 5 pm, a full seven hours before the clock strikes. The road is cordoned off, and the New York City Police Department more or less surrounds the crowd, so you're pretty much herded like cows. There are no in/out privileges, and there's not much to do or entertain you while you wait for the clock to strike.

When we arrived, we moved into the herding area and marked our spot in the middle of Broadway, right in front of the MTV studios. The first hour went by relatively quickly. We were already freezing, but we knew that the temperature would only keep plummeting as the night progressed. For some reason, I thought that a million people standing close by to one another might warm us, yet when I got there, I couldn't even feel my own body heat, much less the person standing next to me! The only relief was that the skyscrapers somewhat blocked the wind. Having to cope with that as well would have been too much.

Occasionally someone from the MTV studio would come to the edge of the window, and we'd look up to see if they were famous. Almost always, they weren't. We had a bottle of whiskey, which we shared, and we chain-smoked cigarettes while we thought about a lovely warm beach somewhere very, very far away.

After the first hour, the night's trials began to show themselves, and our resolve came under fire. It was cold (again) and getting colder. For my friends, the thought of standing there for another six hours seemed too much, especially as Thomas began to feel a natural urge. Unfortunately, there were no in/

out privileges and no toilets inside the corral. We told him to take a leak right there in the crowd, but he decided to hold it. We reminded him there were six hours to go. He sucked it up. Later, when we found an empty champagne bottle near our feet, we offered it to him for use. He declined.

By the third hour, those that wanted to leave became more vocal. At this point, there was a good possibility that some wouldn't make it through the night. I knew I was the driving force behind us being there, but even I considered saying, "Screw it, let's just go somewhere that has an open log fire." Still, I hadn't come all the way to New York City to be warm, so I rallied the troops, and we fought on.

Around then, it became apparent that the cigarettes weren't going to last the night at the rate we were smoking. This was particularly worrying as smoking a cigarette was the only somewhat active thing we could do to help pass the time. We did a count of everyone's cigarettes and figured that if we rationed, we could each smoke one cigarette every 20 minutes. This seemed an easy proposition, but we eagerly anticipated every cigarette for the rest of the night. By the way, Thomas was still holding it.

Shortly before the halfway mark, Tim felt his bladder tighten up while I wasn't far behind. We marvelled at Thomas holding his composure since he'd been going through the ordeal for two hours more than us. I don't think either Tim or myself held it for longer than 30 minutes. I knew I couldn't hold out until midnight, so it was either leave now or figure something out. Tim looked around at his feet and found the empty champagne bottle from earlier. He relieved himself satisfactorily with a million people around us, and I followed suit.

Urinating into a champagne bottle took a certain amount of dexterity. This was compounded by the fact that we were trying to do it while still wearing our coats and gloves. I wasn't even sure if I was going for the first few moments. Then, when

I was sure, I didn't know if I might be missing the bottle altogether and simply leaving a massive stain on the inside of my coat. Eventually, you felt the warmth through the glass, though, followed by the utter relief that something good was happening in your body. After it was all over, I was more than happy. In fact, I was downright chipper about the whole event. Tim and I smoked our next cigarettes with a relaxing calm that two heterosexual men can rarely have together. We offered the bottle to Thomas. He refused.

I noticed many people leaving by the halfway point, which spurred another round of discussion about whether we should do the same. I told them they could go if they wanted, but I would stay even if I were the only one. My speech showed my friends how much this night meant to me, so they stayed put. There were no further discussions about how prudent it would be to leave for the rest of the night.

At 9 pm, a group of people began to lean into us heavily. Looking in their direction, I saw a small gap appear in the crowd, and at the centre, a woman was relieving herself on the Broadway asphalt! We heard a few cries of shock initially, but they quickly subsided. Really, what could she do? After all, it wasn't as if she could use the champagne bottle! In hindsight, she turned out to be a pioneer. Within an hour of setting the example, women squatting in the middle of the crowd became a common occurrence; we merely took a step to the left or right to make sure we weren't standing in the spillway. Broadway had indeed turned into a cesspool of alcohol, cigarette butts and urine. Even our champagne bottle was now on its side, contributing to a Times Square River.

As the night drew on, MTV studios put on a little entertainment. Green Day performed a short gig, and from time to time, famous people appeared at the window, increasing in numbers as we got closer to midnight. By now, I, for one, would have been entertained by two guys' thumb wrestling.

The second half of the night seemed to go by a lot faster. It might have been the increased energy around us, or maybe we were no longer looking at our watches. Whatever it was, anticipation was swelling.

During the last hour, the sound of whistles, shouts, music, and the general expectation was a great crescendo, New York City at its best. I've been there a few times since, and something that always strikes me is its infectious, overflowing life. The neon signs, taxis, people and high-rises all contribute to ambient energy that recharges batteries just by being close to it.

When the crowd started shouting the final countdown, my legs twitched and began involuntary jumps. As the clock struck midnight, fireworks shot from Manhattan's buildings, blinding us for an instant. The crowd yelled, "*HAPPY NEW YEAR*," and memories of watching this exact celebration came back from my childhood. The sky above us was holed between the skyscrapers like a South American chasm. Confetti rained down upon my face, so I stood still and tried to take in as much of it as possible. As I came round, my friends and even strangers were all smiles and kisses towards me, embracing a grateful soul that had achieved a life goal.

Afterwards, the crowd dispersed amazingly quickly, especially considering how long they'd waited for it. Thomas, showing the discipline of a good dog left at home all day, was somehow able to hold his bladder for the entire time and sauntered off to a restroom. As we walked away, I sang Prince's, "Tonight I'm gonna party like it's 1999…" as apt a song as I could think of.

Since that year, I haven't been back to Times Square for New Year's Eve, and I no longer feel the need. That freezing night was like a rite of passage that we performed. It's enough for me to know that I've done it once.

No other New Year is quite like it.

The Worst Hangover, Ever

Mo, Germany

MANY MOONS AGO, WHEN I was a spotty teenager, I went to a party on a farm that would change my approach to every party I'd attend after that. When I think back to it now, I'd consider this the closest I ever came to living like Tim Bukowski. For those of you who haven't heard of Tim, he was a drunken author who pissed many people off.

I'd been super excited about this party for months, so before I arrived, I'd constructed a freakishly large joint that I wanted to share with the guests. It looked so impressive that I christened it my Weapon of Mass Destruction (WMD). A large part of my state shall be attributed to this.

When the Saturday evening came around, I drove to the farm, checked in two hours early and fastened my seatbelt by necking a few beers, followed by a few tequila shots. Even though it was only me and a few others at this point (including the host, who hadn't started drinking yet), I was already quite hammered and thought it a great time to go outside and fire up the WMD. This turned out to be a mistake of gargantuan proportions.

I lit the fuse, and after the others wimped out early, I smoked the entire thing myself. It did destroy me, so at least it was aptly named. Now, as anyone who's been there themselves knows, being extremely drunk and stoned at the same time is neither a good nor a wise move, and it often leads to instances in life that you'd rather forget.

After finishing the WMD, I heard a bizarre noise coming from a large nearby shed. The noise got me strangely excited, and as I peered through a gap in the panels, I couldn't believe my eyes – it was full of bulls. I stared at them in dewy-eyed amazement and thought it would be hilarious to go inside and ride one.

I wandered in recklessly, climbed the side of the enclosure and picked out my lucky beast. I leapt off and landed on it, but it bucked angrily and threw me off as soon as the animal felt my weight. I landed painfully on my side in a few inches of sludge and water before quickly scrambling to the side, so I didn't get kicked. I clambered back up the side panels to catch my breath and heard the others laughing uncontrollably outside. My jeans, sleeves and back were covered in a wet stinking muck, and I suddenly remembered heavy rains from the past week when it dawned on me - it was rainwater mixed with the combined bodily waste from the group of bulls. I sniffed my sleeve and dry wretched because I was covered in watery shit! I had no change of clothes in the car, so, in a hazy moment, I just thought I'd fudge it and hope none of the other guests minded.

After drinking a couple more beers, we headed back to the party, which was now in full flow. So, reeking of faeces, urine, and with unsightly stains all over my clothes, I walked in completely battered and feeling like I was having an out of body experience. I must have thought that the guests wouldn't mind talking to a guy who looked and smelt like he'd been rolling in manure and urine. Needless to say, it didn't take long to work out that people don't want to associate with this kind of guy during their spare time. After 20 minutes of failing to attract anyone's attention, plus noticing that most people were trying to stand as far away as possible, the host asked me to leave. Being way over the legal drink-drive limit, I decided it best to sleep in my car for the night, which was the only sensible decision I made that day.

I woke up the following morning more disorientated than a blind man in a maze. I couldn't remember what had happened or where I was. When I ran my tongue around the inside of my mouth, it tasted like a skunk had farted a few times before dying underneath my tongue. My head pounded with a worrying ferocity and felt like it was cracking my skull open.

I couldn't understand why I was sitting shivering in my car and wearing just a pair of wet, stained underpants. I wiped some mist from the window (with a suspiciously filthy hand) and looked out to see the damp farm and its shed. Memories of the party began to filter back. Memories that would appear in countless nightmares over the years to come. I was freezing but couldn't understand why I'd gone to sleep in just my briefs. My teeth chattered uncontrollably as I held my throbbing head.

The first thing to do was find the source of that nauseating smell. After a fruitless inspection of the car, I opened the boot to find the disgusting wet jeans and jumper, bringing back awful memories of the bull riding incident. With no other clothes to wear, I was faced with a morning-after decision that I wouldn't wish on anybody. Wearing a sour grimace, I pulled on the cold, urine-soaked, shit covered jeans and jumper. That feeling was dreadful and embarrassing - the kind of feeling you never want to go through again due to your drunken actions.

I climbed into the driver's seat with a squelch, opened all the windows, and drove away from the farm without looking back.

MUSIC ADVENTURERS

Tub-Thumping Diaphragms
Ciara Hoey, Dublin, Ireland

IF I HAD TO PICK the most memorable event I've ever attended, without hesitating, I'd say it was the Northern Hemisphere's largest annual gathering, the Berlin Love Parade. Billed as a house music demonstration that promoted tolerance and respect between nations, it was just a good excuse to party hard for most of us on that sweaty day in July 1997. All one and a half million of us.

That day, Berlin's Tiergarten was overrun by the young and hedonistic. If you were old (and had any sense), you evacuated the city. But if you were young and Irish, you decorated your house in Love Parade posters, shopped for the most colourful outfit in all of Berlin, and counted down the days on a giant Love Parade calendar.

Well into the spirit of 'larging it up' German-style, there were pre-parties, post-pre-parties, funky techno after-parties, outdoor events and indoor events. Then there were superstar DJs, random people spinning tunes from the back of their vans, and French fire twirling oddities walking around my house that I didn't even know. It sounds hair-raising now, but it was all accepted without hesitation back then.

I hope you'll understand if the details are a little hazy. The Love Parade is not a procession but an amalgamation of fuzzy events brought together and decorated by feather boas, cloned Gatecrasher teenagers, bubbles, gelled hair, glow sticks, and bikinis, PVC and buffalo boots. The details will probably elude me until my mid-sixties, but my foggy memories include debauched grannies, genuine hippies, freaky German technophiles and all-around good eggs.

And while I'd rather beat myself to death with my own severed arm than listen to techno for 48 hours straight these days, back then it sounded terrific. It probably had something to do with the music being loud enough to vibrate our diaphragms and watching concrete bounce under the weight of Nina Hagen lookalikes and their frenzied Berlin two-steps. And it was hot. It was mind-bendingly, road-wobblingly, shoe-meltingly HOT. Layers were disappearing at a rate of knots, and the whole place soon disintegrated into some urban Woodstock cloth-less debacle. Our Irish mammies would have been praying for our souls had they known the kind of debauchery we were immersed in.

If I only give you one example of the festival's spirit, please let it be this. My defining moment was witnessing the police standing on their van, giving it some to the music while spraying the baked revellers with their water pistols—the frigging Polizei, for Christ's sake… ahhh, only in Berlin (sigh). Anyone who ever accused the Germans of being a humourless race had to eat many humble pies that weekend.

While the event has been much maligned, geographically moved, and even halted in recent years, all I can remember back then is the good. For that week in Berlin, it was all about the young, the messy, the pleasure-seeking and the colourful. Everyone participating wore a huge smile, the atmosphere was more infectious than Ebola, and the city throbbed with the energy of music lovers from around the globe. Music lovers who partied non-stop for the purest purpose, the love of a hard techno beat.

Scooter summed it up best when he said, "I'm raving, I'm raving."

My First Glastonbury

Bob, Epsom, UK

I FIRST WENT TO GLASTONBURY in the late-1990s and then didn't miss another one for over 15 years. It's a weekend I live for and a privilege I hope to continue until I'm a withered old man, collecting my pension and saving towards the next ticket. When I think back to it now, it's funny that this obsession was conceived with a single moment of green-eyed jealousy in my local pub.

While our best friends were leaving for a sunny two-week Mediterranean holiday, a penniless Rik and I weren't going anywhere, and we were being made well aware of the fact. Without realising, drunken promises began to form at the end of my tongue.

"We don't care that you've got two weeks of hedonism in the sun... because... hic... me and Rik... well... hic... well we're gonna find our own party... at... Glastonbury... yeah, GLASTONBURY... you heard right... aren't we, Rik... Rik?"

He looked at me, shrugged, and returned to his pint like a mysterious sea captain who'd agreed to sail to undiscovered lands with a nod. Despite Rik being an easy recruit, the guy was an oak, had a dark sense of humour and would be a solid companion for the weekend. And just like that, in a cornerstone of time, I was about to embark on a lifelong adventure.

The following morning I called a few friends I knew would be there. They said that if we did get in, then we should aim to find a stone circle, climb the nearest hill, cross the stream and on the left, we'd find a massive dragon where they'd be camped. Stone circles and dragons? It sounded like they were going to a medieval re-enactment, not a music festival. We decided to chance it by heading straight to Glastonbury and working out how to get in once there.

Twenty-four hours later, we felt a burst of excitement as we left Epsom on our big adventure. The sun shone gloriously, and with a youthful exuberance, we cadged a lift to the motorway, where we stuck our thumbs out for half an hour before someone took pity. We spent the next four hours getting lifts from various tradespeople and van drivers until we ended up somewhere near Winchester, realising that our last driver was either a complete arsehole or had no sense of direction.

Our saviour arrived in the form of a vacuum cleaner salesman heading home to Cornwall. He was more than happy for us to drink and share stories, to the point that it was a sad goodbye when he dropped us off in the dark two hours later. He wished us well and said that he'd have joined us if he'd been ten years younger. The lights of the pre-festival gave off a warm glow yet still looked so far away. With no map, our only option was to walk as the crow might fly, so we crossed fields and passed through villages before reaching a closed off-road. As we approached the barrier, a policewoman turned and seemed surprised to see us coming from her guarding area.

"Oi, you two," she shouted. "What are you doing in there?"

We stood sheepishly, not knowing what to say, and she asked to see our tickets. We still stood there, hands in our pockets, glancing at each other and looking even more suspect. Eventually, she laughed and said,

"Oh, I see, you're planning on a ten-pound tunnel, are you? Go on, the festival's that way!" We took our cue to leave and hurried off in the direction she pointed.

Twenty minutes later, we made it to the daunting walled perimeter that we'd have to go over. It was high, and we were short, like Jack at the bottom of the beanstalk. We found a quiet spot and sat on our rucksacks, waiting for something magical to happen. It didn't take long for a dodgy bloke and his twitchy girlfriend to appear out of the bushes claiming to be the veterans of this kind of thing. They hadn't missed a festival in years and said we should follow them if we wanted to get in.

We walked and walked, tracing the fence's perimeter and crossing small streams on rotting pieces of wood. We walked through rutted fields, and a couple of times, I lost my footing and fell, but like a trooper in festival training, I righted myself quickly to avoid losing sight of our new friends.

At one point, we heard a low hum, closely followed by a revved engine. We jumped into nearby bushes, and nobody dared breathe as a spotlight shone all around us (unfortunately, I'd crouched on a huge nettle patch that stung my arse without remorse). Eventually, the vehicle sped away, and I swore aloud, cursing my bad luck for a stung bottom; however, the veterans said that nearly getting caught had been a blessing in disguise. In their haste to hide, they'd stumbled on a large log that the four of us leant up against the wall. Within minutes we'd clambered up our saviour and dropped into a sparsely populated Glastonbury Festival field. After a quick check to make sure we'd not been seen, we disappeared into the inviting darkness of the festival.

It had been a long day, so immediately, we set about erecting our tent, rewarding ourselves with a smoke and a well-earned rest afterwards. At midnight we climbed inside while our two new friends slept on the grass outside. As I lay there grinning, I wasn't to know that I'd go on to recall this day a hundred times over in my future.

I woke to a crisp morning and peered out to see if the veterans had survived the night. One was asleep outside, the other nowhere to be seen. After an hour, I crawled out of the tent and forced my feet into cold, damp hiking boots. The festival was now open, and people had begun to arrive, erecting tents everywhere; some in small clusters, others arranged in circles cordoned off with sticks and tape.

Leaving Rik to sleep, I started walking and, after 100 metres, was overlooking a valley where the heart of the festival and its huge domed tents and extravagant stages stood. Tents and parked cars were hives of activity on the surrounding hillsides with revellers setting up. It was my first actual festival moment, and as I soaked it up, it dawned on me that I was a part of something massive and historical, something with a power and energy that had surged before and would surge again. Hundreds of new arrivals streamed past me, lumbering an array of items from deckchairs to barbecues and blow-up dolls to crates of beer. They carried heavy backpacks and muddy tents, some dragging shopping trolleys laden with wellington boots, wood, air mattresses and iceboxes.

I followed my friend's instructions and found the stone circle, closely followed by an enormous stone dragon. It wasn't long before we were reunited, and they'd even saved us a plot to pitch our tent. By 9 am that morning, we'd upped our sticks and resettled.

And then the rains came.

The skies opened for four days and four nights, and it chucked down. As the festival got underway, paths turned first to slush and then to a sticky mud attached to you. But no matter how deep the mud got, the festival kept moving up through the gears. Every musical style you could imagine was represented: punk, techno, rock, jungle, metal, house, folk, classical, jazz and others I couldn't even tell you.

Those dressed in eccentric and outrageous costumes became dirtier by the hour until they were entirely caked in mud. This didn't matter to them or anybody else; we were all in the same quandary (or quagmire). Bands, t-shirt vendors, DJs, market stalls, takeaway vans and huge speakers were always in our line of sight.

The main stages hosted superstar names, while minor acts played in a hundred other venues for some to discover and others to support. A unique cross-section of society danced under the festival's spell, and the worse the mud got, the better the festival got. I watched as England defeated Colombia in a World Cup football match shown to dozens of cheering supporters on a projector in a small marquee. Later that evening, I ate lentil stew in a tepee. Looking back now, I was in my prime, and it was one of the best weekends of my life.

Whether it's Glastonbury or wherever, a festival is a unique entity. It attracts all walks of life, mixing them into a weekend of freedom, celebration and debauchery. Average Joes set tents up next to people they'd never usually mix with back home, then quickly become friends. So what if someone has a tattoo on their face, wears skintight black clothes, or lathers on funky make-up, the festival's crowd concentrates on enjoying music and freedom to party like one.

Whether it's in mud, sun, or in a messed up stupor, Glastonbury is a beautiful and inspiring place. Like Brigadoon, it appears out of nowhere and disappears almost as fast, leaving an indelible imprint on the minds of those who witnessed it. It's a break from modern life, a weekend away from work, from worrying, and all the other crap that makes life tedious and programmed.

But more than this, it's a holiday away from yourself.

How To Make An Old Man Happy

Hannah Bower, London, UK

BEFORE I TRAVELLED, I WOULDN'T say I liked dancing. I guess it's because I'm self-conscious and never felt comfortable shaking my booty while people might be laughing. Now that I've had a few unforgettable moments, my view on dancing, like many other things that govern my self-consciousness, has changed considerably. Sometimes it takes just one moment to shift a barrier like this, and mine came on a sunny afternoon in Vietnam.

We'd just finished a long boozy lunch on a party boat when our crew began acting suspiciously. They docked at an island and asked all the revellers to step ashore before quickly transforming our bench seats into a stage and then rigging up an electric guitar, a microphone and a set of drums using some plastic water containers and a rusty oil drum.

What unfolded was comic genius as they each took up instruments and began to belt out Vietnamese interpretations of various western classics. They played Waltzing Matilda in Vietnamese and English, followed by a funky rendition of Jailhouse Rock. The lead singer became increasingly possessed by a drunken, melancholy Elvis as the song developed. Time and again, he tried unsuccessfully to coax the female audience members into dancing a jig with him during each piece. Though the entertainment was splendid, none of us dared to become Elvis's leading lady.

A couple of songs later, I noticed that an old man with a wooden leg had mysteriously appeared on the boat and was jiving away in the corner. He was going at it with such verve that he could have had three legs rather than one. It turned out that the old mover lived on the island we were moored at and was the alcohol supplier for our party.

Well, he must have seen me looking over because when Twist Again came on, he made a beeline directly for me. With a surprisingly stern grip for a pensioner, he yanked me up on stage and began to twist with a vigour I didn't think possible, especially with one wooden leg. Everybody watching began to laugh, which was mortifying at first, but after a few moments, I thought, 'Oh bugger it,' and gave it everything I had.

You're probably thinking, why do I suggest you do something similar? Well, from the moment I stopped caring about how I looked, dancing with him became so much more fun, and once people realised that I didn't care, they too got up and began to shake their booties. I danced like nobody was watching, and I realised how free it made me feel. It was a short but definitive life changer.

Naturally, it provided a few interesting photographs, and one of them still sits on my mantelpiece to this very day. It shows me with a crimson face, a rear-end sticking in the air, and a spirited old Vietnamese dance partner on one wooden leg looking like he's back in his heyday.

To say he was legless wouldn't be fair, but he was. And so was I.

HIKING ADVENTURERS

The Roof Of Africa
Belinda Goode, Tanzania

TWENTY-ONE HOURS LATER, SITTING IN a leaking tent with rivers of mud running through our front porch, I can now unravel the longest and most exhausting night of my life. I haven't slept for 36 hours, haven't eaten in 24 hours, and haven't walked as far in all my 27 years as I have today.

I got no sleep before we set out due to excitement, nerves, nausea, uncomfortable temperatures, and a pooh with stage fright that didn't want to appear. This was in complete contrast to my tent-mate, who was snoring so loudly I thought the glacier above us would break off.

Harold, our stoic assistant guide, called to our tent at 11 pm, which was a sign to don all our warm clothes in anticipation of minus 20-degree temperatures at the top. I climbed out of my sleeping bag and put on two pairs of thick hiking socks, tracksuit bottoms, combat trousers, *four* t-shirts, a long-sleeve t-shirt, a woolly jumper, a fleece, and a waterproof jacket, two hats and two pairs of gloves.

The push started well, and our energy and breathing were fine as we trekked in the moonlight, a new concept that added an air of mystery to our world. An hour in, and all we could see above us was a long and disparate line of head torches, other poor souls tackling their own night of suffering.

Most of the summit attempt involved switchbacks where we climbed the mountain's gravel in zigzags. It was about half-way through these switchbacks that all our group reported heightened symptoms of altitude sickness. Our guide told us the section we were on would take roughly three and a half hours, but having mislaid my watch, I had no concept of time. In its place were dizziness, headaches, exhaustion and a heel injury, the last of which made me extremely grateful that I'd invested in a good pair of hiking boots, and I still had the advice repeating in my head like a mantra:

"Always spend money on a good bed and a good pair of boots because if you're not in one, you're in the other."

How I'd have happily swapped the boots for a bed at that point.

After struggling for three or four hours, we were elated to find the ground become far steeper, which we took as an indicator that we were close to the rim. However, our head guide Josephud crushed these thoughts, telling us we still had another hour of switchbacks before reaching the 'very, very steep gravel' (as was also worded in our guide book). This statement deflated us, and a few of us looked resigned to not making it to the top.

I can't speak for the others, but I tried to shut out all pain, focusing solely on putting one foot in front of the other like Frodo in the Lord of the Rings. After I stumbled three times at the back, I heard two of the guides talking in Swahili, and my name popped up. I took this as a sign to move up the line, urging my entirely worthless body to push through its exhausted resources.

With half an hour to go, we heard faint cheers from climbers ahead of us who had just reached their goal. Those bastards, I remember thinking. Their pain is over.

A stunning sunrise appeared behind us next to Mount Meru, and knowing it was almost within our reach injected optimism that we could make it, bar any more of those God-forsaken switchbacks!

The last push didn't seem as terrible as predicted, possibly because we now recognised the top after many false peaks. Despite my utterly battered state, I almost jogged the last twenty metres. I yanked off the gloves, grabbed the camera and took a video of our half-dead team with their thumbs in the air.

As I panned across, I captured a boiling hot cup of tea being filled to the brim by Josephud, zooming in until I could see the steam rising from the top. I had to pack the camera away and get my gloves back on quickly; my fingers were losing their senses, and the camera wouldn't be far behind. It was almost cold by the time I picked up my tea, signifying that this environment indeed was lethal.

Reaching the top of Mount Kilimanjaro was a moment so uplifting that, for a while, we struggled to speak. Through hugs and a few choked back tears, we collectively agreed that it was the most physically demanding experience any of us had ever been through.

It was one of the most beautiful moments of our lives.

Many Have Walked, But How Many Have Truly Experienced?

Harry Panton, Edinburgh, Scotland

SOMETHING SHOCKED ME. I WAS desperately tired but fiercely alert at the same time. There was movement around my tent as bags were packed and boots strapped. I had walked 35 kilometres in the past three days - not much for some, I agree but try walking it at altitudes of up to 4200 metres through freezing clouds, then down steep gullies to 1000 metres where the jungle passes are so humid that your clothes become damp. You will feel discomfort, I guarantee.

Thousands have completed the world-famous journey to Machu Picchu, but how many have submerged themselves in what the experience is about?

The camp was all but dismantled. Those from my hiking group had departed, and I was left solo at camp number three. Beer from the night before, a lack of oxygen, no breakfast and impure water had all taken their toll on me. I struggled from my sleeping bag, wrapped up warm, packed my things and began the final leg of my hike to the Lost City of the Incas.

It was 4.30 am, and dawn was kept at bay by the steep Andean mountains. To fully understand how remote we were and to appreciate the achievement of constructing the Inca world, I planned to try and walk in their shoes. I could have been one of the many messengers who streamed the mountain routeways, delivering tidings from rulers on high or passing offerings to the Gods. I could have been a soldier sent to reinforce garrisons under siege from Hispanic invaders; I just had to grasp the scenario. I was in the middle of the Andean jungle, pounding my feet against vast slabs of limestone rock carved into cliff edges, linking the remnants of one of the greatest civilisations this planet has ever seen.

Sheer drops to my right would have taken me to certain peril. A thousand metres below was a babbling river which at one time offered direction to searching tribes, while above were the lush peaks that had looked down on the rise and fall of a mysterious empire. Shimmers of light appeared against the cloud, painted onto the night sky. Thicker bands of cloud moved in fast. By 5.30 am, I reached the Sun Gate, the first offering of the unfinished capital of the Inca people. It is not understood why the city and its complexities were not completed, just wondered.

I stood in awe as clouds peeled away to reveal Machu Picchu. It was lit up by the morning's first rays shimmering through mountain passes, radiating visions of what might have been. Having no idea of direction other than to follow one of the ancient paths, I stumbled off in the vague direction of the fabled monument. Llama's appeared out of the thick fog and began their breakfast of thick grass, dripping with dew.

A sign pointed toward Machu Picchu, but as new steps began, I wasn't convinced I was taking the right path. The granite craftsmanship was tireless - immense blocks had been laid as steps, and I felt its beauty perhaps defined a purpose or route of importance. Eventually, sure that I wasn't on the right path, I settled into the hope of finding a different treasure.

I must have been the first to choose the route that day as I broke the cobwebs shielding my path. Onwards and upwards, the steps led me, my knees becoming weaker and lungs heaving as oxygen became increasingly more valuable. My lack of sleep, combined with the deprivation, increased my anxiety. I climbed for an hour with no sign of any companions and a starved view due to the encroaching fog. The path below and above was lost to thick swarming blankets of cloud. Strange thoughts sounded in my head as I felt I was reaching places never seen before. The steps continued, and as I forced each step from my feet, the surreal ambience encouraged havoc in my mind. The peak had to arrive soon, surely.

Finally, I stumbled across a clearing in the rock and heather and, at long last, glimpsed the flag that I had seen from another valley the previous day. A trademark rainbow shone as my chosen treasure. I could see nothing of what I had achieved, but I knew I had just climbed Mount Machu Picchu on my own, before 7.30 am, and without realising what I was doing.

I stopped to soak it up. The air was cold and thin, yet refreshing. Sweat froze as I perspired, and all I could hear were the sounds of birds, insects, rivers and waterfalls. Valleys stretched out on all sides as I sat and watched everything before me. The clouds broke, and the mountain drifted in and out of my imaginary void. Way below me lay the former Lost City of the Incas. I tried to capture the emotion that might have passed through the mind of the great American explorer Hiram Bingham when he discovered this site shrouded in jungle.

The marvels have since been revealed to all, but to those who still seek mystery and fascination, gaze upon the old fortress from a perch up high. I was constantly amazed those few days, and none more so than when I stood at the top of the Inca world.

What Happens In The Bush, Stays In The Bush (2004)

Humphrey Clegg, Melbourne, Australia

AT 14 YEARS OLD, THE teenage mind works in mysterious ways. It's a time when the home is a place to escape, and the bush, the forest and the mountains are the perfect places to go. I didn't understand my desire to leave the city, only that an urge was felt as if it came by accident. In an attempt to escape my teenage angst, I first fell in love with the forests and bush of Australia. The where and when is unimportant.

Unlike many, I enjoyed school camps. They extracted me from society and took me far away, usually to the outback where we walked 25 or 30 kilometres a day - quite a distance when I think of it now. I trekked across mountains, traversing ridges and tracks so deep that I could appreciate the fleeting nature of my existence and where one wrong step would enlist gravity in the short story of my demise. I crossed cavernous valleys so thick with flora that if I walked up ahead or dropped back behind, it was easily conceivable I was out there alone.

Only I wasn't. My peers were walking out front or behind me; all spread out. Even though we'd known each other's names for years, in a way, we were still strangers. We knew a person on the surface because of a shared schooling experience, but deep down, we knew no more about each other than all our talked-out routines.

However, as the expedition reached its 10th day, changes had become apparent. New friendships had formed, and existing ones had flourished. On the other hand, old friends who previously influenced you no longer did, and they'd shown a weaker side to which you no longer aspired.

We encouraged each other for the most part but at times poked light-hearted fun. As our school intended, we shared an intense experience where we grew individually. Those trips to the bush made men out of some of us. Of that, I am sure.

When it was time for the dreary school uniform to be pulled on once again, the memories faded. Within the camp, though, a wonderful camaraderie of boys acting like little men had existed. There was a shared pride in all of these acts: building, punching, working, smoking, resting, and eating.

When teenagers escape, they also create. They create themselves for a moment as they want to be. Who they are and what they will become are insignificant. In the everyday world, the dream they weave beats itself against our society's physical and social structures. But in the bush, in the forests, on the mountain ascents, walking does not challenge the teenage image; it frees it momentarily.

This is simply a romantic instance. A memory.

ANIMAL ADVENTURERS

Bucket List Number One

Gwen Rodda, Chicago, US

I WAS TRAVELLING THROUGH NEW Zealand when I stopped at a charming little town on the South Island for a few days. Kaikoura was an extraordinary place with a peninsula extending into the sea on its south side, making it possible for a resulting current to bring in all kinds of marine life from a nearby trench.

The town is well known for its crayfish, but many visitors are drawn to whale watching and swimming with dolphins. On top of this, the area brings in many southern fur seals, and an abundance of ocean birds fly overhead. These include the largest of all seabirds, the albatross, which has a wingspan of up to 12 feet!

Arriving here offered an opportunity for me to tick off the one thing that was top of my bucket list – swimming with dolphins. Early on my second morning, I donned a seriously thick wetsuit and dropped off the side of a boat into Kaikoura's bitterly cold and seemingly bottomless bay. As I floated there bobbing like a human buoy, I couldn't see a single dolphin, no matter where I looked.

A friend told me beforehand that the best way to attract them was to sound like I was having fun underwater. Dolphins have a sense of humour, so I put my head under the water and began to shout random noises at the top of my voice. At first, I felt a bit silly, but after five minutes, I was rewarded when a whole pod of them came to the surface, and I almost peed my pants with excitement. I whooped as I swam into the middle of them, diving down to interact and hopefully keep them with me.

I attempted to swim in circles with them but had no idea one would try to mimic me (or at least that's the way it seemed). As it brushed against my torso, I should have been concerned by its enormous strength, but the truth is I'd never felt safer around animals or mammals before. I'd also been told to attempt eye contact with them, another trick to get their attention. This was a little more difficult than underwater noises, but I eventually managed it with one and felt an unrivalled moment of communication between land and sea. This was the closest I'd ever come to communicating with non-humans, which left a deep impression. After 30 minutes, I was worn out, so I spent my final few minutes simply floating there with my face down as they curiously swam around me.

After climbing out of the water, I took off my wetsuit, and my body contracted into itself. The cold wind coming off the water turned my skin into five and a half feet of wallpapered goosebumps! It was the coldest I could ever remember feeling, and back home, I'm used to the freezing winds blowing in off Lake Michigan, so that's saying something.

As I attempted to get warm, my body shivered so much that I couldn't stop my mug of steaming hot chocolate from spilling over onto the boat's deck. Despite my goosebumps, the hypothermia couldn't penetrate my glowing heart. The dolphins had started a fire there that a thousand oceans couldn't put out. My face was glowing from the constant smile etched across it for the whole day, thinking happily about completing my number one bucket list dream.

Pamplona, Irish Style

Niall Hogan, UK and Ireland

"WORKING ON THE FARM SOUNDS like it'll be *great craic*," I said.

"Indeed young Neilly… the craic will be migh-ty, so it will!"

As we drove across the Emerald Isle of Ireland, my cousin Aongus casually dropped into conversation that we'd be stopping by his friend Pat's farm on the way. He gave me the standard sales pitch of it being "Great craic" (crack) which is usually enough for anyone to agree to anything in Ireland. He added that Pat would likely need a hand, and in exchange for plenty of beers that evening, we would muck in to help him out.

It was Good Friday, and alcohol wasn't sold anywhere in Ireland that day, but Aongus finished his sales pitch by saying,

"Don't worry about that. Pat's the paddy, yer man knows a place."

When we arrived at the farm, Pat unceremoniously threw me a pitchfork and put me to work. He was a no-nonsense farmer who commanded I shovel 'enough' barrows of potent manure, however much 'enough' was. I got to work and, over a few hours, slowly made my way through the mound he'd allocated.

As I shovelled, I couldn't help noticing a large herd of bulls that Pat kept in an enclosure nearby. They were ugly and massive, and I remember thinking they looked damn scary. Eventually, I shovelled my last barrowful, so I made my way over to the lads attending to fence repairs. I was shattered and sweaty but proud of my efforts.

"Alright, Pat, mate, I'm done… what's the plan now… is it time for a cuppa?"

"What's dat boy? Yev done both piles 'av ye?" he said.

It turned out there was an even larger pile at the back of a shed he was now pointing to, so I trudged off complacently, my head drooping like a wilted crop. I filled up a few more barrows, fully aware that I'd never make my way through this pile but still determined to earn all that beer in the evening and for the *great craic*.

An hour later, the lads walked over, saying that they needed an extra pair of hands on a job. They handed me a sturdy wooden stick and told me it was time to transfer the huge, scary bulls between two pens. They needed to attend the gates, one at each end, and I was required to help guide the bulls by whacking the stick repeatedly against the ground. They told me to be aggressive with my actions and commands and usher them with a few well-placed prods.

"Don't be scared, young Neilly," said Aongus, reassuring a concerned face. They told me that the bulls were placid animals and would probably shepherd themselves anyway.

I stood in front of the gates, wondering how I'd found myself shovelling shit and facing a herd of bulls on Good Friday. As the gates slowly opened, one bull got wind of what was happening and smashed them wide open with his head. I began whacking the stick and shouting obscenities as though I were a necromancer from the next village, here to drive away evil spirits. The bulls showed absolutely no signs of being neither placid nor slow. They were running, they were mean, and I was in trouble.

Smelling fear, they ran straight toward me with saliva dripping from their mouths. Loud clicks filled the air as hooves pounded the concrete like headless horsemen of the apocalypse riding to take my head. Holding faith, I stood my ground and thrashed the stick. Surely the bulls would come to their senses and realise that running towards the wailing wizard equalled unparalleled danger?

No, it didn't appear that way. When it dawned on my brain cell that they weren't stopping, I dropped the stick and bolted as Usain might. My heart was beating like a cornered mouse as I leapt over the nearest gate into a welcoming pasture. I immediately looked around me, grateful I could see nothing that resembled a bull or even a sheep.

I sat shaking and breathless, feeling the adrenaline coursing through my veins. I looked to Pat and Aongus for their reaction to my near-death experience, only to find them both keeled over. They were laughing so hard that as the tears fell from their eyes, neither could breathe, let alone speak. Those bastards had played me properly. It took a few minutes, but eventually, I saw the funny side and walked over to hear the first of many wisecracks to come my way that evening.

On top of my running with the bulls, that day delivered a second cruel twist of fate. During the late afternoon, I had to assist with castrating those poor buggers, an act that neither the bulls nor I appreciated very much. Still, despite the trauma of these two events, Aongus assured me it would all be worth it when we sat down to some *great craic* and plenty of beer in the evening.

Despite the big sales pitch, when we finished, and Pat took us to his beer man, supplies were running low, and all he could sell us were four tins. My reward for a day of shovelling shit, castrating bulls and nearly dying was one can of beer!

Yes, it had been *great craic*, alright. After I drank the beer, I went to bed scratching my head and thinking that Aongus was indeed a damn fine salesman. He could probably sell *craic* to the Colombians.

You Can't Beat The Smell Of Camel Fart In The Morning

M. K. Wrench, London, UK

INDIA WILL ALWAYS BE THE most magnificent country I've visited. Even though it smells, there's very little basic hygiene, and rubbish is strewn everywhere, I highly recommend it. On top of the dirt, there's a religious belief that cows are sacred too, so with people not being allowed to kill or eat them, they wander the streets shitting and living off a healthy diet of plastic and leftover flip flop foam. It makes for quite a remarkable sight. Despite these oddities, you have to believe me that India is the most extraordinary country.

My friend and I were a month into our around the world journey, entering what we considered a 'finally coping' phase. We'd eaten plenty of dodgy-looking food without meeting the Grim Reaper, though there had been a few lengthier moments of sitting on the can. We'd toured popular tourist traps without getting too upset about paying the hiked tourist prices. We'd even become accustomed to the constant staring and (grudgingly) to the sneaky arse pinchers. And lastly, we'd perfected our answer to everyone's favourite question:

"So, who's your favourite English cricket player?"

Only to be told, "Oh… Nasser Hussein? He isn't English; you do know that, right!?"

So, where did our next challenge come from? Land, sea or sky? What would be the ultimate experience to annoy our friends back home as they slumped over their morning spreadsheets? We found it in quaint little Jaiselmer, a fort city in Rajasthan not too far from the Pakistan border. Here we did what all young women should do when trying to find themselves; we hired a couple of camels and a guide and headed into the desert.

We perched atop our humped friends for three days, routinely waking at dawn to trek in the cool morning air. When the heat became unbearable by late morning, we'd eat lunch and take shelter from a fierce sun underneath scrawny trees with thorny bushes. In the late afternoon, we'd wake from naps, shake ourselves down, and trek through until the early evening, making camp against the familiar backdrop of spectacular sunsets.

We'd settle ourselves in the dips between dunes, shielding ourselves from the cooling winds overhead. In the centre of our caravan, we'd build small fires with scattered wood that was bone-dry, providing us with the heat and light we needed once darkness had consumed everything around us. Under the stars of the world, we cooked fresh chapattis, potatoes in a yellow sauce, and soft rice. Our bedding was made up of swag-style mattresses with warm blankets that we rode upon during the day. Although the blankets had a strong camel whiff to them, not to mention an abundance of moulting wiry hair, we were grateful to be wrapped warmly as the cold winds blew above us, tickling our exposed flesh.

Some aspects of this adventure will never fail to draw sentiment.

Lying on the dunes, staring up at never-ending stars brighter than we'd ever seen.

An all-encompassing nighttime silence, broken only by the tinkle of a camel bell, snore or fart!

Our zany guide's magnificent nature made us giggle whenever he attempted English, and he never once took offence to it. And whenever things got a bit quiet, as they often did, he'd liven them up with his improvised and animated camel races.

And, of course, the camels.

Mr Lalu, my friend's steed, had a naughty streak and always wanted to be at the front, biting whichever camel was in his way to get there. At one point, he made my camel jump three feet into the air simply by sizing up the exact right spot for a nibble and causing him a maximum fright. Mr Lalu had also perfected the original snotty look and reminded me of a 2-year-old with a permanent cold.

And then there was my camel, Niko, who stank. Niko had a farting problem – he didn't know when to stop! He'd fire one-off if anyone ever approached from behind just to let you know he was around. And those farts had such gusto that he could have been in an orchestra. Standing in the wrong place when the wind carried one of his guffs was as far from a breath of fresh air as you could imagine, and he was so effective at playing the anal tuba that he almost knocked the guide out with a rasper at one point.

However, by the end of the trip, I realised that a powerful camel fart was the perfect remedy to a groggy head in the morning.

Niko in F(art) minor had become the desert's warped version of paracetamol.

A Tale of Two Elephants

Paras Purohit, London, UK

"MR PARAS, WOULD YOU LIKE to meet your elephant?"

Your elephant. Not words you hear every day, but precisely the ones I wanted to hear that day. An elephant has the most remarkable memory of any animal on the planet, and I hoped that mine would still remember me if we met again in 40 years.

I'd hopped off the bus near the Chang Thai Elephant Camp at 9 am, full of giddy excitement about the mahout course I'd booked. However, after looking at the sign again, I'd gotten off the bus 2 kilometres too early! My backpack weighed over 35 kilos, and the temperature and humidity were already creeping up past 35 degrees. Now I'm no marathon runner, and this wasn't going to be pretty.

I shuffled in the direction of the camp, and it wasn't long before my clothes were soaked right through with sweat. As I climbed a hill along the way, droplets slid down off my nose and face as I felt the energy drain from my bones.

I first saw Chang Thai Elephant Camp at the summit, spread out in all its glory and sparkling like a hidden gem in a forest. I stood there exhausted, soaked, and probably smelling like an elephant, but my wide eyes were filled with beautiful adventures, like a scientist spotting his first Brachiosaur in Jurassic Park.

Something about elephants has a profoundly calming effect on me. They represent what I feel we as a species should be: intelligent, strong, non-threatening and innocent. Sure, an elephant is a territorial animal, but it doesn't have an inherently mean streak like we often do.

I stumbled down the hill and into the camp's reception area, dropping my bags with what sounded like a permanent thud. Walking over to the receptionist, I said, "Sawadee kap," and bowed my head slightly, the masculine Thai greeting for both hello and goodbye. I dabbed my forehead and straightened my crumpled shirt with a regimented yank, somewhat embarrassed by my appearance. She replied with "Sawadee ka," the feminine.

I explained that I meant no harm despite my appearance and was booked onto a mahout course. She looked me up and down, laughed a little and then made a call to someone else, laughing down the phone to them too. It didn't take long before a Thai man in his late 20s walked through the door and offered his hand.

"Hello, my name is Pat. Did you get off the bus too early? You are very sweaty! I understand you want to do mahout course? We really cannot at the moment as elephants very tired… but there is one elephant, I think, and as you booked already onto course, we will do it… ok?"

Well, thank buggery for that, if only because the 2 kilometre walk back to the highway would've killed me. I told Pat I was beyond grateful and filled out the routine paperwork, including a disclaimer to say I wasn't allowed to sue them if an elephant sat on me and other clauses of a similar nature.

"Come with me now; I will show you your house," he said.

Pat dressed in trousers and a short-sleeved shirt, making me think he was a conduit between the tourists and mahouts. If he was a mahout, he certainly didn't dress like one, and as we walked through the camp, he asked if he could help with my bags.

"Even your little bag is *sooo* heavy," he laughed as he hauled it onto his slight frame.

We dropped the bags off at a small thatched hut that looked like it might collapse under a hefty sneeze, but he told me it was standard mahout style housing. Then he casually said,

"Mr Paras, would you like to meet your elephant?"

My elephant. Nobody else's.

"Yes, Pat. I would like that a lot".

He took me to a large open showground area with logs and tools scattered around, where two tourist shows happened daily. At one end was a viewing area filled with wooden benches and in front of these stood a colossal elephant with a tiny man the size of a boy perched on its neck. We headed straight for them.

"Mr Paras, this is Khun Bun," Pat said as he gestured toward the lithe older gentleman. Then he turned and spoke to Bun, introducing me as "Mr Paras."

Khun Bun literally hopped off the elephant like an olympian and landed equally gracefully; then we bowed to each other while saying, "Sawadee kap." His clothes were worn, and he didn't have anything more to say, but his broad smile radiated enough warmth to make up for the lack of words.

"And this, Mr Paras… is Than Thuan," Pat said, pronouncing it 'Tan Too-wan', as he walked towards the fourth and by far largest member of our party.

I could say that this first meeting was awe-inspiring, but I was terrified. An elephant is a hefty animal, and a good-sized Asian elephant can weigh anywhere between 2.5 and 5 tons. Even though I am slightly rotund, I don't hold a candle to that, and Than Thuan could have snuffed me out before I'd have stolen even one banana from her. If she took a wild, instinctive dislike to me, she could easily wander over, pick me up and play a little frolf with me.

"Shouldn't it be golf?"

"No, Jerry… frolf… frisbee golf." I'm a big Seinfeld fan.

As Pat stroked her trunk, he casually motioned for me to climb onto her. Surprised, I took a step backwards and tripped over a log. I'd just committed a cardinal sin for a guy not wanting to make sudden movements. I stammered to Pat that I needed a little time to become comfortable with my newfound friend before climbing on top of her. I introduced myself with a few pokes and graduated to friendly pats around her face and trunk. She blinked as I touched her, and this continued for quite some time before Pat said that maybe the mahout course wasn't for me. Oh, was that right, Pat? Was that right? Well, we'd see about that.

Bun demonstrated how to climb onto Than Thuan's back while Pat reassured me that nothing I did would harm her. For her to lift her ankle, I had to kick it lightly and shout, "HAP SOONG," then put my right foot on that ankle, grab her ear and haul myself up in one swift movement. It was easy. Bun demonstrated it twice more. Easy.

My turn.

Or not so easy, as it turned out. Bun was a tiny man, lithe and flexible. He'd been climbing onto elephant's heads for 25 to 30 years. Mr Paras was not so tiny, nor lithe, nor flexible, and he'd never climbed onto the head of an elephant. What followed was five minutes of comical clambering all over poor Than Thuan, tugging at her ear frantically while trying to get one fat leg over her enormous head. I did eventually achieve it, but at a considerable cost to my fisherman's pants as it ripped a sizeable hole from my crotch all the way around to my bottom, much to Pat and Bun's amusement!

Learning to be a mahout wouldn't be easy.

For starters, I found the sitting position to be highly uncomfortable. A mahout sits astride an enormous head and uses muscles in the legs and hips that you don't usually use. I didn't even realise I had these muscles until five minutes after taking up the sitting position, and from that first hour, I was in a good deal of muscle pain for a week!

An elephant's head also has tough, prickly hair, which pokes through your trousers into your skin and makes you feel like you're sitting on wire wool. To put it bluntly, I was a human pincushion from the very first moment I sat on Than Thuan.

Still, despite these drawbacks, the view was magnificent. I sat 10 feet high and looked perilously down an elephant's trunk, so I got a great view of whatever was next on the menu (akin to being in control of a hungry vehicle).

My training began with Pat translating Bun's overview of the basics. To turn left, he kicked behind her right ear and vice versa for turning right. Then to get her moving forward, he kicked behind both ears, and for backwards, he squeezed behind both ears. Easy.

My first task was to manoeuvre her through a set of logs in a figure of eight, and it was here, during this relatively simple exercise, that the size of the challenge hit me. No matter how hard I kicked my feet, squeezed my legs, shouted in her ear or gestured in front of her eyes, Than Thuan would not move. This lasted for about 10 minutes until Bun took pity on me and walked her around the figure of eight. He walked, and she followed. He talked, and she listened.

The training, if you want to call it that, was me pretending to guide her, while in reality, she just followed Bun. We went through a list of translated commands, all of which fell on deaf ears when I repeated them. Maybe Pat was right, and I wasn't cut out to be a mahout. Than Thuan certainly didn't think so as I kicked behind her ears while she was already walking forwards (Bun liked that one).

Than Thuan followed Bun's commands without question until any food came into sight, and when it did, she made a beeline straight for it, and there was very little that Bun (or anyone else) could do about it. Yes, Than Thuan's appetite and will were oversized, even by an elephant's standards. Grass, leaves, bushes, berries, branches and twigs were all on the menu for her, but it was bananas that she went bananas for.

"Oh, Than Thuan, eat too much, eat too much... Than Thuan... eat too much," was all Bun would say, neatly translated by Pat.

I could see that the friendship between Than Thuan and Bun was an intimate one. They'd been working together for 15 years and, in some ways, were like a couple, just without the bickering. They were unconsciously aware of one another's movements, strengths and weaknesses, which became increasingly apparent as I took in their small interactions. An elephant's skin is so thick that most insects can't pierce it, but a horsefly has such sharp teeth that it can penetrate an elephant's skin in certain areas, usually around the head and the neck. These parasites constantly pestered poor Than Thuan, and as I sat there brushing them away for her, I wondered how many times Bun had done the same thing. No wonder she took such good care of her friend.

In the late afternoon, the three of us walked Than Thuan to a river, and Bun suggested that I might like to bathe her. I comically scrambled onto her neck and tried to guide her into the river. In reality, she adjusted to autopilot and walked in as though I was a fly who happened to have landed on her.

The water came up to just under the top of her back, leaving a dry area where I perched. Pat told me that elephants like to take care of their mahouts, and I could detect this by the way she sprayed water lightly on her back, making sure I had enough to wash her but keeping me dry at the same time. When we left the river, I was a little wet, but if I told you I'd just washed an Asian elephant, you'd have thought I was fibbing.

Later that day, after we'd walked Than Thuan back to the paddock, Bun tugged at my sleeve and pointed to a large pile of bananas. Usually, I'd have taken this as a sign to indulge, but with Than Thuan around, I thought better of it. At first, I tried to feed her two or three bananas at a time, but she quickly grew impatient with my approach and began to grab entire bunches.

"No Than Thuan, be good, don't grab," I'd say like it would make a difference. In her eyes, I was simply a conveyer belt that took bananas from the floor to her trunk, and the faster I did this, the better!

"Oh, Than Thuan, eat too much, eat too much... Than Thuan... she eat too much," Pat would say as Bun stood there smiling and shaking his head.

Before we went our separate ways that evening, Pat casually mentioned that I'd be taking part in a scheduled elephant mahout show the following morning.

WHAT!?

"Pat, haven't you been watching today? I can't get Than Thuan to move forward, let alone perform in a show! She'll probably eat the popcorn of people on the front row!"

Pat listened to my obvious terror and laughed, assuring me that everything would be fine. He said to ensure that I got plenty of sleep, as I looked like I'd been dug up from the ground. Cheers, Pat.

The following day I woke to Bun's smiling face poking around the door and immediately felt nerves kick in. For the next half hour, I lay on my back, wondering how I could skip the show. Could I feign a muscle injury or call in sick? Perhaps I could grab my bags and run into the forest without looking back. No, Pat thought the mahout course wasn't for me. I would rise like a phoenix from my bed and show him I could handle the mahout heat.

I got dressed, grabbed a banana and left the hut, ambling while contemplating my fate. I liked my elephant, but she didn't listen to me, and our friendship hadn't blossomed as I'd imagined. Still, she was my elephant, and we were in it together. I would do my best to see the experience through and pray that the crowd was a forgiving one. The sweat began to spread again, enveloping my clothes quickly and giving me the look of a panicked man.

I arrived outside the showground, and Pat was standing there next to an elephant that wasn't Than Thuan. I was confused.

"Mr Paras, meet Pom Pwang. She is your elephant for the show today, and she is very well behaved elephant," he said as he stroked her trunk.

Pat told me that Pom Pwang was the name of a famous Thai singer, but his words barely registered as I went through yesterday's lessons in my head. Pat smiled and nodded as if he'd read my thoughts, encouraging me to mount her so he could take me through the moves again. As we went through them, Pom Pwang responded perfectly to every command, and with it, my anxiety faded.

Pat flashed me a grin and gave a thumbs up, saying he thought I was ready. We walked Pom Pwang into the showground where the benches had already filled up with tourists, and as they introduced the riders, I heard 'Mr Paras' called out, my first bow to the world as a mahout. I waved to the crowd and dismounted with optimism.

The show started with five elephants in a row, the other four accompanied by professional mahouts. As each pair was called out, the mahout shouted a command, to which the elephant raised its trunk and bowed to the crowd. I gave my first command to Pom Pwang, and she was right on the money as she bowed.

We dropped our mahout sticks for our next trick and asked the elephants to pick them up. Pom Pwang delivered again. No direction I gave her was too much, and she even played dead on cue.

We moved through the gears, and before I knew it, we were up to our final piece, a potentially tricky Jungle Book-style dismount, sliding down her trunk. I took it slowly, and with her wiry hair jabbing into my legs all the way down, I just about pulled it off. Thankfully I remembered to wear my best fisherman pants (without a crotch hole) that morning, as two trunks for the crowd would not have been a pretty sight! The audience clapped and cheered, and I almost felt like a mahout.

With our part of the show complete, I took a seat in the stands next to Pat, and we watched as the elephants worked together to move logs and tools in an impressive display of brain and brawn. Pom Pwang had been a true professional to work with, making me realise why Than Thuan hadn't been allowed to participate - she was just too naughty to take commands. Still, we'd spent a memorable day together, and I was hopeful that maybe she'd remember that.

After the show finished, it was time to get going. I walked to the hut, packed my things, and looked around the serene forest. It was the perfect place for an elephant.

At the front gate, I said goodbye to Pat, and he told me that Bun was with Than Thuan in the forest, probably eating bananas. I dropped my heavy bags at the gate and went in search of my elephant one last time. I found her nearby; Bun perched high up on her neck, so I held out a final bunch of bananas, and she stuffed them greedily into her mouth.

I stroked her thick skin as her trunk came down and fell around my shoulders, reciprocating the gesture.

Elephants are still my favourite animals, and sunflowers are my favourite flower.

SPORTS ADVENTURERS

The King Power Miracle
Neil Hogan, UK and Ireland

I WAS 13 YEARS OLD when the bug first took hold. It was 1991, and my arm was in plaster as I visited Filbert Street with my friends to watch Leicester play Oxford in the season's final match. Leicester's Foxes had to win to avoid relegation to the third tier of English football, something they'd never experienced in their whole history. Meanwhile, about a mile away from the stadium, King Richard III was lying buried beneath a car park, and he'd been there for more than 500 years. But we'll get to that later.

Inside the ground, we stood in the infamous Pen Two. It was beside the away fans in Pen One and a place where hardy fans chanted while starting the odd fire on the terraces. It was a chaotic and unruly place where anarchy ruled. Once it filled up and the crowd began to sing, I felt a surge of something inside.

Thanks to a Tony James goal Leicester won the match 1-0, sparking a pitch invasion at the final whistle, which most of the fans joined in with, myself included. The feeling that you were a part of something historical shared between thousands of people was palpable, and I was hooked. Any Foxes purist would tell you that I was an extremely fortunate lad to have had this as my first match. I was about to start my football adventure.

I'd grown up playing for Liverpool in the school playground, always pretending to be the goal-scoring machine Ian Rush or captain fantastic Kenny Dalglish. I never spared a thought for Gary Linekar, Leicester's golden boy and the golden boot winner at the recent 1986 World Cup. Liverpool won just about every competition, so we always fought over their players. Little did I know back then that the team I'd marry was literally on my doorstep.

I often wonder how much time, money and energy the most hardened sports fans pour into their teams. I wouldn't consider myself even close to their levels of devotion, but my love and loyalty are respectable nonetheless. For more than 25 years (I'm now in my 40s), there haven't been many matches where I've not in some way expended time, energy or money. Even when I've been in the deepest, darkest, most remote parts of the world, I would often do my duty to get hold of an old dial-up modem and find out what was going on, even if it was 3 am rather than 3 pm!

And when it comes to important events in my past, I often remember them based on what was happening with Leicester City. What was I doing in November 1993? That was around the time Iwan Roberts signed for Leicester and scored two on his debut versus Wolves, so I'd have been visiting my brother in Bedford. How about January 2006? Oh yes, that was when we came back from 2-0 down in the FA Cup to beat Spurs 3-2, so I was in Jodphur, India. And sadly, where was I on Sunday, 4th May 2008? Well, that was a hellish day I shall never forget. I'd just arrived in Panama when I saw Leicester relegated to the third tier of English football for the first time in their 124 year history. What a bloody awful, rotten day that was.

And during this time, there have been some wonderful, incredible moments that I've been present for and never felt more alive.

Like standing in Pen Three with Dean Anderson when Leicester went 2-0 down against our local rivals Derby after only 10 minutes. Nineteen minutes later, we led 3-2 through Iwan Roberts treble. Dean lost one of his shoes in the melee of Leicester's third goal, and we never recovered it, so he hopped all the way home that April evening in 1994!

There's been quite the relationship with the Championship play-offs over the years, and back in the 1990s, Leicester played an unrivalled four times in the final. This annual match is now known as 'the richest match in world football'. The prize money and spin-offs stood at £170 million, according to Deloitte in 2017. In the 1990s, even though the money was nowhere near this level, it was still the culmination of 49 matches and had the ultimate prize of entry to the Premier League in front of 80,000 fans at Wembley Stadium.

My friends and I were never more nervous than in the build-up to those finals. Our first visit was in May 1992 when David Speedy dived for a penalty, and we lost 1-0 to Blackburn Rovers. It was enough to make me cry. The following year we returned and played Swindon Town, who went 3-0 up before we fought back heroically to 3-3, with Steve Thomson's equaliser being one of the best feelings I can ever remember. Then we lost 4-3 to a late Swindon winner, and I'm sure I cried that day too. Whether or not you believe in fairytales, the following year was exactly that. We went back for the third year running and finally won 2-1 against Derby County, with our long-serving hero Steve Walsh scoring both goals. We were back in the Premier League, and our fans were delirious with excitement. Sadly, we only dined at the top table for one solitary year before being relegated again.

It was a blessing in disguise as there followed five wonderful, life-changing years with our eccentric Northern Irish manager, Martin O'Neill. During a turbulent period in 1995, he steadied the ship and got us promoted again on his first attempt. Once again, it was via the play-off final, and this time it was against Crystal Palace. Our enigmatic striker Steve Claridge shinning in a half-volley winner in the last minute of extra time, and the Leicester half of Wembley stadium erupted like nothing I'd ever seen. I remember looking to the heavens and screaming, "There is a God, there is a God." It was my second greatest footballing moment, but we'll get to my greatest soon.

Martin O'Neill followed this up with four top-ten finishes in the Premier League, plus three League Cup final appearances where we won the competition twice. Considering we'd only ever won the cup once in our whole history (1964), this was an incredible feat. O'Neill took us as far as he could, and he'll always be remembered as a total gentleman, a great comedian, and a leader of men.

I could go on with the memoirs, but I wrote this story because of a modern-day miraculous adventure that my fantastic football club created in 2016. Most of you reading this will know exactly where I'm heading, but please do allow me to recap the facts.

In 2008 we were relegated to the third tier of English football.

In 2009 we won the third tier and got promoted back to the second tier.

In 2010 the club was purchased by a Thai company called the King Power Group, owned by a gentleman named Vichai Srivaddhanaprabha, or Khun Vichai (or The Boss) as he affectionately became known by the fans.

For the next four years, we knocked on the door of the Premier League each season. This included a depressing moment where we missed an injury-time penalty against Watford, only to see them go up to the other end of the pitch and score a winner 10 seconds later, condemning us to another year of heartbreak. I witnessed grown men sob after that one.

In 2014 we finally won the second tier and got ourselves back into the Promised Land, the Premier League, setting a new club record of nine successive wins. Stay with me now because this is where it gets completely bonkers.

With 29 games of the following 2014/15 season gone, we had merely four wins to our name and were rock bottom of the table, looking like dead certs for relegation. At this point, whether or not it had anything to do with it, King Richard III, who'd been discovered buried in a car park next to a pub in Leicester a year prior, was given a regal burial at Leicester Cathedral. He was the last British king to die on a battlefield and the only king whose remains were thought lost. From the day after his burial, we began an incredible run of winning seven of our final nine games, avoiding relegation and finishing the season as one of the best performing teams in Europe.

Then, at the start of the 2015/16 season, we weren't quite sure what to expect from the Foxes, especially with a new eccentric Italian manager in the shape of a potentially washed-up Claudio Ranieri. What we witnessed, however, defied logic. Before we even kicked a ball in August, the odds against us were 5000-1 to win the Premier League, plus Claudio himself was the bookmakers' favourite for being the first manager to be sacked. Despite this, we began where we left off from the previous season, winning plenty of games and only getting beaten once. By October, we were down to 1500-1, and then by November, we'd dropped to 100-1.

During the December of that season, my wife gave birth to our beautiful daughter, and at that very moment, Leicester

City was sitting top of the Premier League. Two hours later, we weren't, but that was ok; when she entered the world, we were, and history states it. We'd unbelievably gone down to 10-1 with the bookmakers by this point.

Over the years, I've moulded myself as emotionally guarded, so it took a while to think we could win it genuinely. However, that moment came on 6th February when we visited a strong Manchester City team and demolished them in their own back yard. The score was 1-3 to Leicester, but anyone who watched it will know that 4-0 or 5-0 to Leicester would have been fair. It was time to start believing, so I projected the end of the season onto my plans and realised I'd be in California with my wife and daughter during the final vital matches.

And so it came to pass that on 2nd May 2016, a day that was also our 2nd wedding anniversary, Leicester had a chance to win the Premier League. We were in Sonoma and had just booked into our elegant wine country hotel to watch Spurs vs Chelsea, praying that Spurs didn't win. And thanks to Eden Hazard's 82nd minute stunner, they didn't, sending us into spasmodic celebrations.

Alongside marrying my incredible wife and the days our beautiful children were born, it was one of the most fantastic days of my life. I never even remotely thought it was possible. In 132 years, we'd never done it before, and then we did it with the odds of 5000-1 against us. This also meant they'd won all three of England's top professional divisions in just seven years, something I doubt will never be done again.

As the staff and guests wondered what the screams were coming from our hotel room, it's hard to describe how I felt. My palms were sweaty during those dying moments, I felt nauseous, and my hands shook. Finally, once it was confirmed that we were champions, I felt one of the most incredible lightning bolts.

"We've done it, we've done it… I can't believe it; we've actually done it."

I jumped around screaming in ecstasy, kissed my wife and baby daughter, and shed a tear. Afterwards, the adrenaline coursed through my veins so vigorously that I didn't stop shaking for an hour. It was only 2 pm local time, so we had the opportunity to celebrate all day, tasting local wines, eating cheeses and walking around with a Leicester scarf draped over our baby buggy as strangers honked their horns in recognition.

At times I still can't believe it all happened. I wonder if perhaps there are multiple parallel universes, with this one being the only one where Leicester won the Premier League.

Whatever universe we're in, though, this one states that between King Richard III being given a ceremonial burial in Leicester and the end of the 2016 season, we only lost four Premier League matches out of a possible 47 and that alone is the foundation for a modern-day phenomenon.

Tragically, two years after our King Power miracle, Khun Vichai died. He was in his helicopter along with four others as they took off from our stadium following a match and crashed immediately outside the ground. Nobody survived. We couldn't believe the images unfolding on our screens as our blue hearts cracked into thousands of tiny pieces with each breaking news story. It was the darkest day in our club's history, only two years after its brightest.

Vichai's death brought everyone who loves Leicester City even closer together as we grieved side by side, those thousands of tiny pieces being the fans coming back together to create one massive fractured blue heart. We were incredibly blessed that this gentleman ever came into our world and created the best memories any football fan could ever desire.

Vichai laid the cornerstone for us to go on and achieve our dreams.

Claudio and King Richard simply guided the miracle home.

The World's Best Stadium

Joe O'Hegarty, Birmingham, UK

RIDING THROUGH MELBOURNE IN A taxi, I once got into a conversation with its sprightly driver about the world's best stadiums. Being in his early sixties, the guy had global experience and a strong opinion about it. He told me excitedly that he'd stood in his fair share of "Bladdy good ones, mate", but none that had ever captured the energy inside his city's very own Melbourne Cricket Ground or MCG as it's more commonly known. Being a thoroughbred Melburnian, I naturally applied a particular bias to his opinion. Still, as his reasons unravelled, it became difficult not to be charmed by what he had to say.

Through smiles and trailing eyes, he recalled when he'd watched the Rolling Stones play a fantastic sell-out concert way back in the 1970s, with the crowd harvesting a high that, "Ya jast down't see no maw, mate". Then he laughed and added about the numerous occasions when Australia had spanked the English cricket team on Boxing Day and the days that followed. "Or yih mate, fair dinkum, we always went mad for thouse."

Surprisingly, his most memorable experience of the MCG was a "Bladdy soccer match". I say surprisingly because he confessed he wasn't much of a football fan, and his decision was based purely on how raucous he'd seen the crowd. The match in question was Australia against Iran in a World Cup play-off game, where the winner progressed to the World Cup of France '98.

He said the Australian fans were so giddy with excitement that if they'd acted in unison, they could've blown the ball into the back of the net. Getting a bit jerky behind the wheel at this point, he shouted back to me that there were roughly 100,000 Aussies fans in the ground, compared to 200 Iranians being drowned out in the corner. Of course, he was exaggerating, but he told the story with such verve that it didn't matter. I was sold on visiting his shrine.

And it didn't disappoint.

As I walked into Melbourne's cauldron, the atmosphere was electric Aussie banter, and the stadium was a three-tiered spectacle. I bought tickets for a local derby in an Australian Rules football match, Richmond vs Collingwood, two Melbourne neighbourhoods that border each other. In fact, of the 18 teams in the AFL, half of them are from Melbourne, which shows how much the city goes into meltdown for 'Ozzy Rules'. The game was unanimously one-sided, with Collingwood thrashing Richmond's britches, and though I knew little about the rules themselves, I was motivated by generosity to sing for both teams.

A guy in front of me sang heartily too. A guy with the most unforgettable mullet I've ever seen, which personified the 'business in the front, party at the back' look. The guy was a true blue Aussie, and at one point, I became more interested in watching him eat a meat pie than watching the game itself. By the time he'd finished, he had a third of it sitting in his moustache like a character from a Roald Dahl book (aka Mr Twit). I laughed until I felt like I'd punctured a lung.

The MCG was an impressive stadium and an absolute must for any sports purist looking for a unique venue to watch a match. As I sat with my supercharged Aussie brethren, I thought back to the taxi driver and our conversation, grateful that the seasoned old pro had offered the recommendation.

And going back to the result of the football match he'd mentioned, well, with 20 minutes to go, Australia were 2-0 up and had one foot firmly planted in France's World Cup. Then, in a total capitulation that their fans could only describe as they "Shat their duds mate", they lost their heads, let in two goals right at the death, and Iran qualified on an away goals rule.

He told me that when the final whistle went, "I never 'erd 200 blokes sand like 100,000 bifaw, cobber!"

Confessions Of An English Football Patriot

Peter Burns, London, UK

LONDON FOG IS A MYTH from Sherlock Holmes. Still, cold air descending on the Alps often makes the whole of the vast plain of Lombardy, from Turin across to Venice, a danger zone for driving or any other outdoor activity for that matter. And the outdoor activity on this shrouded November evening was a friendly football match between the English and Italian sections of a multinational firm.

As a fit twenty-something, I was invited to make up a team of not so fit and not so skilful employees. The match was in anticipation of the 1976 World Cup qualifier between the two nations and an excuse to get together and let our imaginations run wild. Not that a raw, dusty, fog-shrouded pitch on the industrial outskirts of Milan was likely to conjure up thoughts of Brooking and Keegan or Causio and Bettega.

What scattered patches of green there were, revealed themselves on closer inspection to be a few surviving, hardy weeds that spread their tendrils widely enough to give the illusion of grass. It was a surface that had long since surrendered to the inevitability of a dust bowl or quagmire, with the occasional interlude of untameable vegetation.

The team kit was a loaned set of rugby jerseys with long sleeves and collars, not ideal for imagining you were a silken-skilled midfielder but perfectly acceptable for a two-degree Celcius Milan night.

As an effective old-style centre half when a schoolboy, I harboured dreams that I'd missed my real role in life and that the PE teacher had pigeonholed me too early. In what was effectively an international match, I controlled the midfield with a combination of well-timed interceptions and tackles, followed by surging runs and delicately weighted passes. This was real enjoyment, and I wasn't going to let that yelping Italian, who I'd robbed of the ball a couple of times spoil it. '*Vaffanculo*' to you too, I said, trying hard not to rise to his provocation.

I managed to do this for a while until, having just pulled the ball down on my thigh - God had I improved - and sent it looping over the back four to our galloping striker, I was thumped in the back by my yelping nemesis. I didn't snap but just turned and half-pushed, half-cuffed him as more of a gesture. Within seconds dust and weeds were up my nose as the two of us scrabbled on the halfway line. In an instant, the other players were pulling us apart and holding us back – not that I needed any holding back; like most playground fights, I was relieved when people intervened. So relieved was I that after we'd both given assurances that it wouldn't happen again, I took a step towards him and offered to shake on it.

Cultural differences are plenty between Italy and England. For instance, please and thank you are not needed as much as in England, never let another car through in Italy, getting pissed is bad for the image over there, Italians have never worn loon pants, and so on. However, the reaction to my shake-on-it was to leave me gobsmacked, almost literally, as he lunged at me with another '*Vaffanculo*'. We were soon both on our way to the touchline for what was my first ever sending off. I felt embarrassed, especially as I'd been asked to play as a guest, and was also frustrated that my greatest moment as a midfield general had been cut short.

This match was, after all, a friendly. It had nothing at stake aside from pride, and the twenty-yard walk to the touchline seemed to have given my nemesis time to reflect on this. All it needed were a few requests from the players to the referee and repeated assurances from the two of us that we'd pack it in, and we were back on our way to midfield. Absolution. Back from the dead. I trotted towards my opposite number, hand outstretched to emphasise to all my penitence…

'*Vaffanculo! Bastardo! Figlio di puttana!*' He was at it again.

Ten seconds later, I was sitting on the bench with an equally astounded English spectator, contemplating what might have been and also what cultural idiosyncrasies had contrived to get me into this situation. And it wasn't finished yet, as every time their winger passed the bench, he shouted something, which in my confusion, I took to mean that I'd hit him first.

This situation having happened in Italy, excuse me while I digress briefly to mention the similarity between this situation and Francis Ford Coppola's best undiscovered film, 'The Conversation'. I won't spoil the movie for you but will simply tell you that the intonation of one word changes the whole plot and outcome. So it was to be, on this foggy night in Milan, as the change in intonation clanged into my consciousness. In Italian, the indefinite article 'una' – *a*, and the number 'una' – *one*, can both be the same thing. As my new teammates came over to the bench at halftime, and I protested at how crazy my nemesis was, their winger came over and repeated, 'Lui ha una mano' (*he has a hand*).

I realised, this time, that the stress was not on the 'lui', but the 'una' and that 'He has *a* hand' was not some veiled threat but meant to be taken literally, word for word. Perhaps I hadn't heard him well the first time, but he added the word 'sola' this time. 'Lui ha una mano **sola**,' (*he has **only** one hand*).

After the match, the opposition said he was extremely upset at how it had gone for him, and it was better that I didn't wait for him to get changed; they'd explain my translation faux pas. Anyway, as one teammate suggested, it probably wasn't worth waiting for him to get changed and put his hook on!

As it goes, we did meet again, some two months later, before the return match. He trotted up to me, and we shook hands this time…. left hands.

FOOD AND DRINK
ADVENTURERS

The Last Supper
Mark Cox, Bedford, UK

IN THE LAST YEAR OF university, I lived in a shared house with five hungry guys, so our kitchen - which wasn't even big enough to swing a mouse - was always a bubbling hive of activity. Dinnertime was often a spectacle. Arms reached through arms to stir hot pots of bubbling beans, lurched through legs to snaffle cheap packs of instant noodles, or opened the gross fridge door that would dig into someone's back as the culprit searched for an industrial-sized tub of butter, which held more crumbs than butter.

It was typical of a student house shared by five blokes, so eating around dinnertime was only easy if you had something on toast, hence the crumbs in the butter, I guess. However chaotic the kitchen's state, our industrious flatmate Marlon managed to cook a traditional roast dinner within its walls at least once a week, every week.

As the end of semester two loomed on the horizon like a dark cloud ready to pour down some realism, our time in the house drew to an end. We'd been a close unit for three years, always looking out for one another and always looking forward to being reunited after trips home during the holidays. This time there'd be no repeat of it, though. We'd all be going our separate ways. But before life whisked us away to be shat upon by corporate society, Marlon proposed the idea of cooking one last huge traditional roast dinner together, aptly named The Last Supper. We agreed immediately.

Word went out that it was going ahead, and suddenly 14 people wanted in, which posed a slight problem. How did we cook an enormous roast dinner in a pokey kitchen where it was a struggle even to make a pot of rice? Our project manager Marlon navigated this by recruiting two other cookers, one next door plus another half a mile down the road at a friend's place. He was on a mission to produce a lunch that would go down in the annals of history, and as student meals go, the planning and delivery of The Last Supper were Michelin-starred.

The main event came around quickly. It was a Sunday, a sunny day, and the second day of the Euro 2000 Football Championships. Between shopping, cooking, dishing out orders to his henchmen, and communicating with the other kitchens, Marlon ran the show. When he initially took the project on, I was sceptical about whether he'd survive it without having a nervous breakdown. Still, I was delighted to watch our resident head chef manage three kitchens as smoothly as he did.

At 1.30 pm, we sat down to a veritable feast. As we cast our eyes over the table, they took in three chickens, two sides of beef, a joint of pork, 12 different types and styles of roasted and steamed vegetables, pigs in blankets, Yorkshire puddings, stuffing, and a bucket (yes, a bucket) of gravy. It was reminiscent of a story where a king's lost prodigal son returns with the most lavish banquets held in his honour. Since waking that day, we'd been fasting and were eager to tuck in, which was evident by the four attendees who'd brought large plastic trays to replace their plates!

By the end of the meal, the table was such an amalgamation of colour, texture and unconventional mess that it resembled a piece of artwork from the Tate Modern. One by one, people fell away from their plates (or trays), dazed and confused through excessive eating. Most went to fall outside or collapse watching the football on a sofa, though inevitably, all fell into a food coma. With the sun beating down, it had all the gloss of a Christmas Day in Australia.

When the evening arrived, we built a small fire on the stones in our back garden and brought the sofas out to sit and reminisce over three joyful years. We got hungry again (especially Hungry Henaghan), so we wrapped pieces of meat and potatoes in tin foil and threw them into the fire to cook. It was like we were starting university all over again.

It's been over twenty years since The Last Supper, and inevitably we've all moved on to different places in our lives. Sadly we've not managed to gather the group together for a reunion since, so it stands in the memory as a timeless day. One where we considered our highs and lows, joys and tears, the friendships cultivated and those who'd dropped out. We joked about the first times we'd all met and the subsequent journeys we'd travelled.

We were graduating, not just from university, but from an unforgettable three years of life. Time would bring us new episodes that contained travels, careers, mortgages, marriages and kids. But before those adventures began, it was our way of saying goodbye to one another, and it was a fitting end to a defining chapter.

Loire Valley '98

Bobby Ahn, Austin, USA

ON MY LIST OF THINGS to do before I die is 'To drink a glass of wine in the Loire Valley.' I'm not sure why this particular challenge is on there, though. I originally intended my list to motivate me to visit these places, so in theory, I could have just as easily said, 'Go to the Loire Valley and sit on a chair.'

Why the area was so appealing, I don't know. I must have recalled something a former French teacher had said about it or seen a picture of a chateau and become enamoured with the architecture. Regardless of what it was, I wrote it on my list that way and was determined to get to the Loire Valley when my chance arose. That opportunity finally presented itself in the summer of 1998, while I was in France for the Football World Cup.

The Loire itself is a river that cuts across central France, winding through hills and villages and lined with spellbinding chateaus in the valley. This picturesque place embodies all of my best thoughts about the French countryside. The Loire Valley, the most beautiful section of the river, is also known for its wine.

I boarded a train to Tours with my travelling companion, Todd, to get to the valley. We didn't have many passengers in our section, only ourselves and a crabby, elderly lady who gave us dirty looks from time to time. At one point, while we were stopped, I decided to have a smoke. When I stepped into the corridor, I noticed a local guy smoking next to the

'*Ne fumer pas*' (no smoking) sign. The signs appeared regularly down the length of the corridor, but the Frenchman didn't seem phased. For some reason, I felt compelled to ask the question anyway.

"Fumer ici?" *(Smoke here?)*

"Bien sur!" *(Certainly!)*

I wasn't sure his answer would save me from the conductor kicking me off, but I figured, 'when in Rome…'

When I returned to my section, I was surprised to see that our congenial old lady had miraculously transformed into a beautiful princess. It might have been this way, but it was more probable that the elderly lady had gotten off when our new companion had got on. Sitting opposite, I couldn't help studying her profile a little. She was young (I guessed in her early 20s) and had straight brown hair with shy brown eyes. We glanced at each other a few times before striking up a basic conversation with my limited French.

I learned that her name was Aline. She was 20 years old and a student from Lyon heading towards a small town near Tours, which coincidentally was the same place we were heading. By the time we got to our destination, we'd enjoyed each other's company so much that we agreed to meet the following day in a local park. As it goes, we'd spend the next three days meeting at that park. We mainly spent our time having laboured conversations that required significant effort from both sides, but we seemed to communicate enough to keep meeting up.

We spent the first day lying on the grass under the warm afternoon sun. Later we went to a café for a sandwich, followed by a pot of coffee and a bottle of wine. As we drank the wine, I talked freely and let my grammatical mistakes happen. When I poured the second glass, it suddenly hit me that I was ticking off something from my list of things to do before I die. The café wasn't a chateau, and neither were we in view of the river, but I don't see how that could have made my memory of the experience any better.

All I knew was that I was striking off a challenge on my list in a way that I could have only ever dreamed of. I enjoyed my Loire Valley glass of wine in the company of a charming, beautiful French lady.

C'est bon.

The Global Language Of Absinthe

Neil Hogan, UK and Ireland

TRACE YOUR LIFE BACK, AND you'll see that certain decisions will have led you down specific paths. Life produces extraordinary, sudden instances that forever change how we walk its trail. Moments that shaped a person's life profoundly can be overlooked; moments that perhaps seemed trivial at the time but were significant in hindsight. From a successful interview leading to happiness in your current career to getting hit by a cupid's arrow at a party you weren't supposed to attend.

Ending a lengthy relationship in my early twenties was one of these. It led to a desire to escape reality and brought about a trip to Prague to do it. It was February 2001, and I flew there with my friend Jas, a bear of a man at the time, standing at six feet one and weighing in at over 125 kilos. He has a deep laugh, plenty of jokes in his locker, and strangers feel comfortable around him.

On our second day, it was my 23rd birthday, so we went to see the magnificent Prague cathedral, walking up the 200 or so steps and feeling double our age as we panted like the hung-over tourists we were. Afterwards, we had a delicious lunch of chicken filled with mozzarella cheese and salty green olives, a side order of fresh crusty bread and a breath-taking view overlooking the city.

We had nothing more planned by mid-afternoon, so if you're a believer in fate's plan, then this is where it came into play. It was the point where we met the Americans. In life, paths may cross only once, but once is enough to change time. At the bottom of the steps, we found a side street; down the side street, there was an alleyway; at the bottom of the alleyway, there was an Irish pub, and outside the Irish pub, there was a sign saying 'Live Football'. In our eyes, Pub + Football = Happiness, a simple equation for our afternoon.

Inside we ordered a couple of pints of Czech Staropramen beer and sat at a piano in the corner to watch the match on a small screen. The pub was old and authentic, and it looked like tourists had been having a good time there for years. Random crazy crap was nailed to the walls (as is compulsory in any Irish pub), there was an array of cold European beers on tap, and the waitresses were smiling and attentive. The front door opened as we sat there, and four smartly dressed, well-mannered chaps walked in. They were each wearing black leather jackets, and one of them spoke to the barman in a deep voice with a solid North American accent, "Hey sir, have you got a big screen in here?" It turned out they did, around at the back.

A couple of minutes later, we picked up our drinks and followed them, and at the back of the pub, we found a huge oak table that looked like it was from the dark ages. The state of it conjured images of extravagant banquets, jugs of mead, hunks of meat, and heated war debates. Down one side sat the Americans, while at the top was an English couple. There was a big screen on a wall at the end of the table, so Jas and I opted for the one unoccupied side. General chitchat ensued between the eight of us, and it transpired that the American lads were Tim, Thomas, Jason and Bobby. They were friends in their late 20s who had studied together at the University of Texas in Austin and decided to do an Eastern European tour as their vacation. Nick and Lucy were an English couple on an anniversary weekend from Leeds in the UK.

As soon as they heard it was my birthday, they were intent on helping me celebrate, even though we were total strangers. Rounds of *triple* absinthes arrived at the table, and everyone had a glass; there was no backing out. It was four against four, the UK vs the US, and we had to outdo our Yank cousins.

With tradition, we caramelised the sugar by dipping a spoonful into the potent absinthe and then lighting it. After stirring it in, the sugar didn't help much, for when we drank, the devil had poured it himself and then farted in our mouths. I may as well have been licking suede for all the joy it gave me. By experiencing the harsh taste in unison, we collectively debated having another one, a ritual akin to watching holy people flog themselves in public. They ordered another round, closely followed by two more. Our mouths became anaesthetised, and our newfound friends didn't let us put our hands into our pockets for the whole afternoon.

In the early evening, Nick and Lucy were due to go for a meal at an exclusive restaurant. To this day, I don't know if they made it, but judging by the way they staggered out of the pub holding onto anything that wasn't moving, I'd be surprised. Entering a drinking competition on their anniversary weekend probably hadn't been the most romantic way to spend a weekend!

Jas and Jason turned the absinthe competition into a personal drinking rivalry. At the final count, Jas managed 18 shots to Jason's 21. There's a photo knocking around of them that would be at home in a Steven King Film Production, and to this day, we have no idea who won the UK vs US drinking competition. We eventually left the pub and wandered the streets of Prague with our cousins from across the pond, soaking up the alcohol with dinner and finally making it to a nightclub where we partied until the early hours.

When we said our goodbyes at 4 am, we promised to meet up the following evening, which was also everybody's last in Prague. There was mutual doubt as to who would show, but both parties did, and we had another memorable evening, this time sans absinthe. On our goodbyes, we swapped email addresses and promised to stay in contact, perhaps even to meet up later in the year. Thousands of promises like this happen on a whim, yet rarely do they come to fruition.

Spending time with folk from a different country had been a refreshing experience for both parties, and we were determined to keep in touch. Six months after that Prague weekend, Jas and I flew to California to visit Bobby before he moved back to Austin. Sandwiched around that, Bobby and Tim visited the UK twice, and the four of us also backpacked in Ireland together.

It was Bobby who I grew closest to. We keep in regular contact to this day, and always will. Born in South Korea and raised in the United States, he has an approachable, honest aura and is an attentive listener (the two ears, one tongue approach). He's widely read and has reasonable, balanced opinions on most things, political and historical. Liverpool FC is one of his biggest passions, and when I first visited him, I heard that top of his bucket list was to sit in the Kop one day watching a match at Anfield. Ten years down the line, we did that. We also backpacked in Australia, climbed Mount Kilimanjaro, visited each other umpteen times in the UK and US, and to top it off, he was a groomsman on my wedding day.

Life can work mysteriously like this. New doors opened, friendships conceived, waters bridged, and experiences created from a chance meeting. A desire to watch football had become the cornerstone of an overseas friendship that would last a lifetime. The big decision of the break-up had indirectly led to the small decision of walking into the Irish pub at that particular time. As we look back over our lives, we'll see other similarities, I'm sure. They don't always involve so much absinthe, but then these are just the variables.

Sadly, Jason died. He collapsed suddenly and unexpectedly with a heart anomaly in San Diego shortly after the Prague holiday. Because of this, it strengthened the affection I have for the memories of that trip. It would be impossible for it not to. We all wish he could have been there for everything we've experienced as friends, and I'll never forget his laughter on that crazy afternoon of absinthe.

High Tea

Anonymous

BLAMING IT ON HER ARTHRITIS, my dear old mother has asked a few times if I could buy her some weed. I'm pretty she's asking in a bid to be a cool parent, though she has always backed it up with:

"You know it's all for research purposes, of course!"

The first time she asked, I was a little taken aback. Old-fashioned parents have brought me up, and my father doesn't even approve of getting drunk, let alone stoned, so I couldn't believe my ears when the word 'weed' came out of her mouth. It made me feel uncomfortable in the same way a conversation about sex with your parents does, and I moved the conversation on swiftly and thought nothing more of it.

The second time she asked, I felt curious and questioned whether she might be playing a joke on me. She assured me she wasn't, which made me wonder if she was feeling left out. Nevertheless, I moved the conversation on again and hoped that would be its end.

When the question surfaced a third time, her persistence paid off, and it was time to act. If my good old mum wanted to get high, who was I to refuse her?

A few days later, I visited a friend known for baking the tastiest hash brownies on this side of the Suez Canal. When I told her about my mum's request, she was giddy about making a sizeable fresh batch.

Through years of perfection, she'd crafted a recipe that combined low calories, a rich chocolaty taste, and a high degree of potency. She was in high demand in our village, and I'd have compared her to Heisenberg had Breaking Bad been around back then. Well, the latest batch was the best I'd ever tried, and after an evening of crisps, giggling, and toast, I wrapped a large portion and brought it home to share with dear old mum that coming weekend.

When I got home, she was sitting on the couch watching TV with my father, so I whispered into her ear what I had, and a mischievous grin appeared. I told her I was placing it in the larder with a cover over the top to keep it fresh. She nodded, still with a grin on her face. I went to sleep and left for work in the morning without giving it a second thought.

Imagine my surprise when I came home for lunch and opened the larder to find the whole slab gone, not even a crumb left! Initially, I thought how rude, but this quickly turned to concern as I realised that if someone had eaten the whole slab, then they'd probably be in a bad way. Only three people could have eaten it: mum, dad, or my sister. I shouted up the stairs to see if anyone was home and heard a groan come from my parent's room.

A moment later, my fears were somewhat abated when mother appeared gingerly at the top of the stairs, looking fried. She was in her dressing gown, clutching a water bottle to her tummy and making noises like a teenager who'd eaten too much junk food. She told me she wasn't feeling too chipper, and when I probed her symptoms, I breathed a sigh of relief at hearing the common reactions to an oversized dose of hash brownie.

Still, I couldn't quite bring myself to tell her that the 'bizarre vision and dreams' she was having were hallucinations of sorts. She quietly admitted having eaten the whole slab, so I sent her back to bed with a large glass of water and left her in the mature hands of my sister, who 'doesn't do drugs.'

We haven't talked about it to this day, and I guess it's one of those times when your parents choose not to remember 'that night', except with us, it's the other way round.

Unsurprisingly, I've not been asked to help with research purposes since.

ISLAND ADVENTURERS

The Hog Father
Roger Vidal, Nottingham, UK

THE GUIDE SCREAMED FOR ME to keep running. I'd come across it at any moment and would need my wits about me. I bounced through the thick jungle, tripping on vines and roots before coming to a clearing where I caught sight of the hairy little beast. It sounded like it had its throat cut.

Have you ever seen a wild boar? I hadn't, not even on the National Geographic channel, so I didn't know what to expect, but it wasn't what I saw. The little thing was nuts, and I mean like it had just been released from a lunatic asylum nuts.

"CHASE IT, CHASE IT," screamed the guide from somewhere behind me, sounding like he was desperate for me to catch his dinner. I pursued it through the trees in my sweat-soaked Laos beer t-shirt, khaki shorts and tennis loafers, but I felt overdressed with the guide in just his flimsy shorts and sandals. Moments later, I could hear the nutter behind me again, with his little boy chiming in, "GO ON, CATCH IT … CAAAATCH IIIIT!"

Back home, I played semi-professional football for a few years and kept myself reasonably fit, so the guide had me mistaken for a natural despite never having done this before. I was convinced he only brought tourists here to do his dirty work and had probably never caught a boar in his life.

I came to my senses, and a smile spread across my face as I realised the situation. I was young, healthy, travelling the world, and caught up in a bona fide Fijian experience, returning to Earth's roots. I was a hunter, I was fearless, and I was going to catch this wild boar, even if it scratched me.

My moment came unexpectedly. I'd chased the boar into an area of thick trees on two sides with a stream on the other, so unless it could swim, it was cornered. The little monster suddenly let out a squeal of acknowledgement that it would have to get past me, Roger the Fearless, to return to its freedom. I turned to the guide and his little boy, but they were nowhere nearby.

"HEY, GUYS… THE PIG'S OVER HERE!" I yelled. No answer. I must have lost them with my new hunting speed, stamina and natural sense of jungle orientation. Oh well, I didn't need anyone's help where I was going. I stood like the Christ Redeemer, my arms outstretched in a welcoming but more likely threatening gesture. The boar was 10 metres away and grunted, so I grunted back, though mine must have been the grunt of an animal with low self-esteem because suddenly the pint-sized bugger decided to charge me! I went from the hunt*er* to the hunt*ed* in two seconds, with the bristling ball of fur now pursuing *me*.

As I looked over my shoulder, I noticed two tiny tusks, which got me thinking, 'Shit, if he catches me, he's going to try and stick one of those little tusks in my bum cheek.' This fed my fear, which fed my adrenaline, which fed my close to bursting heart. Natural reactions took over, and without asking the brain's permission, I was running faster than a minute prior, which I think saved my bottom. Well, that and the small tree that appeared in front of me.

I leapt onto it and scuttled up a few branches so I was just out of reach of those tusks. For the next 15 minutes, I balanced five feet above the ground as that crazy swine squealed at the bottom, hoping I'd fall so he could shank me good. As I hovered there, I inspected his tusks and shuddered at the thought of a filthy dagger embedding itself in a buttock.

"HELLOOOO... CAN ANYBODY HEAR ME? A LITTLE HELP, PLEASE," I shouted into the jungle. Eventually, I heard branches breaking, and the sound of voices followed by hysterical laughter as the guide and his little boy caught sight of what was going on. Surprisingly the boar didn't clear off (it must have really wanted a piece of me), and in an instant, the little boy bopped it over the head with his club, it fell in a heap, and there were no more squeals.

We carried the boar back to the family in the village, looking like the fearless hunters that two-thirds of us were. I begged the guide and his boy not to mention the story to the village, but they thought it was hilarious to heap more embarrassment onto the tourist. And they were right; it *was* pretty funny when I thought about it.

That pig might have wanted a piece of me, but if the truth be told, it was me who ended up having a piece of him.

Kava Makes The World Go Around

Neal Owens, Virginia, US

I NEEDED A PLACE TO lay low for a couple of weeks. Anywhere relatively close to Australia would do, so I asked for recommendations. One place kept coming up - a place where sunsets were abundant and the beaches tourist-free, if you found the right areas. As descriptions of this place kept coming in, I began to imagine myself as a character in The Beach, about to set off to find some secret, hallowed place. I was heading to Fiji.

I flew to the main island, Viti Levu, and took a pick-up to a small rural village called Bukuya, four hours away. Upon arrival, I was treated to a traditional kava ceremony, a daily ritual for many families throughout Fiji. Kava is a natural drink made from kava plant roots, numbing your mouth and putting your mind at ease. The village of Bukuya instantly took me in, a stranger being raised to its bosom as its people smiled, laughed, told jokes, and dished out warm hugs. It was a happy place, especially when they drank kava!

After feasting on chicken curry with eggplant, I asked Moses, one of the family heads, if he'd take me hunting. With a smile that I'd come to associate with his trademark, he said he and his brother would take me the following morning, but first, we had to sleep off the kava. I put my belongings into a grass hut (a bure), and before settling in, I had a quick shower using a leaky cold-water tap. I stood in the moonlight, scrubbing my body with soap and ready to howl at the moon, I was that happy.

I woke groggily to a damn rooster crowing at 5 am, feeling that if we ate it that night, then maybe I'd get a lie in tomorrow. I wandered out of the bure in my underwear, trying to remember where I was. I felt bleary, partly due to the kava and also my recent travel. Moses was already rubbing herbs onto his dog's noses, so I donned a pair of shorts and wandered over to join them. He told me the herbs kept their sinuses clear, making it possible to track wild animals from a distance, so I dabbed some herbs on my nose, and Moses laughed. It was time to hunt.

We carried spears and hiked into the jungle with a horse and a pack of dogs leading the way. We spoke intermittently, possibly because of my presence but more likely because it was how they hunted. I'm sure you don't attract too many wild animals with idle chit chat, so I adopted their silent style and remained vigilant.

We followed the animals for a few hours, finally stopping at a steep ridge surrounded by mountains over a lush green valley floor. Moses's brother leapt onto the horse and galloped around the shelf until he was out of sight; then, every few minutes, we'd hear him shout, '*Umbadulasaaaaaaa*,' a fantastical yell that we'd reply to similarly and which reunited us on the other side. As the dogs began barking excitedly and took off, Moses said we were getting closer to the prey. We followed as fast as we could, though I was lagging, and by the time I'd caught up, they said we'd lost it. The dogs had taken chase now, so we'd wait for them to return, and how long that took would determine whether it had been a successful trip.

With the dogs gone, it was time to prepare lunch, so we split up to collect ingredients. Between us, we gathered bamboo, yams from beneath the Earth, breadfruit from the tops of the trees, lemons, small fiery chillies, and firewood. Moses grabbed three spears, walked over to a stream and jabbed under a rock. I had no idea what he was doing, but it looked interesting, especially when he pulled out a two-foot-long eel! How did he know to look there, I wondered.

Moses started the fire as we peeled the yams. The bamboo was then cut into sections, stuffed with yams, covered with a leaf, and placed with the breadfruit and the eel into the fire. Moses took the leftover pieces of bamboo and carved them into small sauce dishes. He filled them with water, chillies and lemon, crushing them together to make a lively sauce that left a tingle on the lips. Large bamboo leaves were laid out as plates to complete the presentation. It was one of the most remarkable meals I'd ever seen. Even with a cupboard full of ingredients back home, I struggle to make anything decent, so I was astounded to see a full meal prepared like this in the middle of the jungle.

After we finished eating, the dogs returned with blood around their mouths, though Moses said the catch was too far away to retrieve. Slightly dejected, we packed up and headed back to the village empty-handed. As we walked, I wondered what might be on the menu instead - would it be the rooster from this morning, or might it be me? Luckily it was more chicken curry.

Later that evening, after plenty more kava, I pointed to Moses's hand and asked him what his tattoo signified. He said that every time his people broke a bone, they tattooed it because the blood congealed underneath and helped the bone to heal faster. I asked if he'd be willing to give me a tattoo to remember my time in Fiji. He laughed deeply and said in his usual laid-back style, "Sure… tomorrow I give you a tattoo."

The following day, after getting woken by that darned rooster again, Moses took me to a small cave that I imagined was his getaway from the stresses that even his world must produce. It was his very own man cave. Half a coconut shell that contained dark ink made from coconut oil and ashes appeared. He then pulled a long thorn from a tree, picked up a small charred stick, and drew three lines on my upper bicep before mixing the solution in the coconut. I didn't have any existing tattoos and was somewhat nervous, but seeing Moses's demure composure helped relax me.

He repeatedly stabbed me with the thorn and the ink, which was more painful than expected, but tattoos are supposed to hurt. Thirty minutes later, it was complete, and we admired my bloody mess, looking at the tattoo and then at each other with giant grins on our faces. After cleaning my arm up, I was able to see the design clearly, with three blue horizontal lines to signify my acceptance into the village. We couldn't wait to show it off like two kids, and as blood and ink trickled down my arm, we bounced off home.

This tattoo was the most inimitable way I could think of symbolising my time in Fiji - something that was a part of me and would reignite island life memories on a tough day back home. Over the following years, I would trace the lines with a finger and remember the village of Bukuya with its fun kava ceremonies, smiling faces, creative cooking, wild hunting, talented Moses, and more kava. That time in my life holds a special place in my heart.

"*Umbadulasaaaaaaa!*"

EMBARRASSED ADVENTURERS

I Doubt I'll Be Invited To Dinner Again

Art Vandelay, Gujarat, India

I WAS STAYING WITH MY granddad in Rajkot, India, when I woke up one morning with the munchies. It was a common affliction for a person such as myself, and after rummaging through his cupboards, I found four packets of banana crisps, a local delicacy. For those of you who haven't tried banana crisps, you don't know what you're missing. They really are bananas, and they really are crisps. God was very kind to us on the day these bad boys were invented.

After eating three 200 gram bags, my appetite was finally sated, so I spent the next couple of hours resting my swollen tummy. Just before lunchtime, a couple of doting aunts came to visit my granddad, and as usual, they forced bowl after bowl of Indian food upon me. This is pretty standard behaviour in Indian households, where relatives fear you may wither away before their eyes while they're on duty. I went to sleep that night feeling way more bloated than usual, but my body appeared to have coped well with the considerable quantity of food I'd consumed over the day.

In the morning, however, I was not fairing so well. During the night, I had to visit the toilet copious times, and my bum trouble was so severe that at one point, I'd even considered moving my bed into the bathroom, such was the amount of time I was spending on the john.

I felt considerably better (and lighter) in the afternoon, so I shuffled my sore arse downstairs to seek out human company. We had another relative visiting that day, and upon seeing me, she demanded that I had to visit her family for dinner that night. Despite my obvious discomfort, she pressed home that she would not take no for an answer. I couldn't refuse out of politeness, despite my tummy saying,

"Having just suffered a major bout of belly trauma, why are you accepting dinner invitations with such gusto, you gibbon?"

To which I replied with,

"Shut up, tummy. It's a testament to my devotion to food, ok!"

Later that evening, I flagged a rickshaw and endured a seriously bumpy ride to my cousin's house. I felt a few rumbles down below during the journey but assured myself that it was nothing a few samosas wouldn't solve. I entered the family home with greetings for everyone and offered my help, which they didn't need. With that out of the way, I wandered into their living room and flopped onto their lovely comfy sofa, ready for the steady stream of food they'd inevitably send my way.

A few minutes later, I decided it was a good time to ease some of the pressure exerted on my colon by the gas generated by my bowels. It took me an incomprehensible amount of time to compute what had just occurred. Instead of the pleasurable feeling of the expelled gas easing pressure on my digestive system, my mind was registering the unpleasant sensation of sitting on a large amount of liquid substance seeping through my trousers, down my leg, *and* onto the sofa!

I did what any courageous man would do. I decided there and then to run away as quickly as possible, shouting my dinner cancellation as I went. Embarrassment makes you act swiftly and irrationally, whether it's rude or not. I needed to quickly find a rickshaw and get the hell out of there before they got wise to the situation. With my eyes darting around the street, I prayed they wouldn't associate the stain on the sofa with me. What was I thinking? Of course, they'd know it was me. Oh well, I had to escape immediately and make my peace later.

Luckily, finding a rickshaw didn't take long, so I hopped on and squelched into a seat. It was a 25-minute ride to my granddad's house, over bad roads that wouldn't be pleasant on a good day. Sitting there being bounced around in my faeces was not a good moment in life, especially with the driver looking at me suspiciously and probably wondering what the hideous smell was. I did my best to avoid eye contact.

At the end of the ride, I got up and noticed that I'd left a stain on the rickshaw's seat too. Thank God the driver didn't see it, otherwise, I'd have died of embarrassment right there on the spot.

You spend your whole life building up confidence in your body and its senses. Since I was young, I've known when it's a good time to urinate, defecate, burp or even vomit, but an incident like this shatters a lifetime of confidence, turning you back into a child overnight. That one fart left me so insecure that it took three days to build up the courage to squeeze one out again without sitting on a toilet.

My relatives haven't mentioned the stain to this day.

Some Stones Are Best Left Unturned

Liam Walley, Wigston, UK

ALLOW ME TO SET THE scene. It was the night of the stag party, an odd one for me as the guy getting married was my fiancée's father, and I didn't know him that well, let alone any of his big rugby buddies. Nevertheless, I'd promised her my best effort, so I turned up on time for the early evening tenpin bowling.

Slightly nervous, I thought the best idea was to knock back a few swift ones and join the banter. Five pints of strong beer later, the lads decided to start a kitty, so everyone chucked in £50, which lit the fuse. Dirty jokes filled the air while slaps landed on backs with merry guffaws. Drinks began to get crazy with pints flying down and chasers not far behind, so if you struggled to hold your beer, going at the same pace as the rugby lads was social suicide.

We lost interest in the bowling but still needed entertaining, so talk turned to a strip club, which wasn't what I'd been expecting. Who goes to a lap-dancing joint with their father-in-law-to-be on his stag night? I've since had flashbacks of getting there, drinking more shots, losing the guys, wandering aimlessly, and babbling at a few people who thought I was a muppet. After that, there's a scene missing.

The following day arrived and with it the obligatory aches and pains. I woke to a violent headache, a tongue that felt like cracker bread, and I dared not move for the first 10 minutes in fear of vomiting. As I lay there dying, I noticed an unfamiliar pair of jeans on the floor. Maybe one of the guys needed a place to crash, so he stayed over. That wouldn't be so bad. But how had his jeans made it into our bedroom? Who cared? I needed coffee.

I made my way gingerly downstairs, where the conversation with my fiancée went something along the lines of this:

"What the hell happened to you last night?"

"We went bowling and then… well… I can't really remember."

"Why did you come home wearing somebody else's clothes?"

"Erm… excuse me?"

"You came home wearing somebody else's jeans and shoes!"

How in the bloody hell did that happen, I wondered. I walked into the hallway, and sure enough, there was a pair of unfamiliar brown shoes where mine should have been. I went upstairs to look at the jeans, and they weren't mine either, so I picked them up, rifled through the pockets and found the following note:

"Please return these clothes to 67 Dale Avenue.
You were well hammered, mate!"

An array of worrying thoughts suddenly entered my mind. What had happened to my clothes? Why had I taken them off? According to my fiancée, I'd rung her at 2:30 am, slurring down the phone that I'd be home in half an hour. I eventually knocked on the front door at 5:30 am, stumbled in, called the bank and cancelled all of my lost cards. I had no recollection of this.

I debated long and hard about what to do, but deep down, I knew there was only one thing for it - I had to swallow my pride and make my way to the address I'd found. Once there, I'd return the clothes, declare myself sane, and pray that the wallet, phone and clothes reappeared. I went to the car and realised that I'd lost my set of keys too. Bugger.

Though I didn't want to share the story with anyone, I didn't have luxurious choices. I called my cousin Phil and after two minutes of hysterical laughter (followed by him relaying the story to his girlfriend and her hysterical laughter), he agreed to pick me up.

We drove to the prison in the city, which was my last known whereabouts. Neighbouring the prison is Nelson Mandela Park, a small recreational area with a circumference of less than half a mile. We walked the perimeter looking for my trousers but found nothing, so we decided to face the firing squad.

We walked to the house, and I breathed deeply before knocking on the door, although not too hard for fear that somebody might answer it. I wanted to find my clothes, but I didn't want to face a person who might have had to clothe a naked me. A minute went by, and nothing, so I knocked again. Still, no curtains twitched, and no sounds came from inside. I was starting to remember a book I'd read called 'Fear' where the main character loses his hat and then can't remember the last four hours of his life. I was eerily starting to feel like him. The dilemma for the guy is that if he finds his hat, he finds his four hours, and if he finds his four hours, he'll die. So as you can see, it was a bit of a predicament.

With nothing happening, we decided to explore. It was a townhouse, so it likely had an alleyway at the very back, and once we followed the pavement around the corner, we found a side gate. Loving every minute of my embarrassment, detective Phil was determined to solve the mystery and slowly opened the gate as though it was booby-trapped. Quite unbelievably, just inside the alleyway sat my shoes and socks with a pair of neatly folded jeans. I scooped them up and checked the pockets, pulling out an untouched wallet and a set of house and car keys. The phone had disappeared, but I wasn't too worried about that as I got through them like deodorant anyway.

I skipped back to the car with childlike happiness, where I dumped my things and picked up the borrowed clothes to return. I walked back to the owner's house and quickly laid them on the front doorstep, looking as inconspicuous as possible.

"Hello, can I help you?" a female voice called behind me. I had a mild cardiac arrest as it struck *Fear* into me again. Was I about to get those lost hours back? Was this a demon come to take my soul? I looked at her, but she didn't appear to have an *"Oh my God, he's back"* look and neither did she look ready to kill me.

"Do you live here?" I asked.

"*Yeees,*" she said suspiciously.

"Would you mind giving these back to their rightful owner, please?"

I couldn't say the last part fast enough before making the sharpest of exits, and to this day, I still don't know what she said next. I decided to head home to my happy life, resolving never to think about this incident again.

However, a few of my friends heard about it, so I couldn't bury it with all the other stories they don't know. As a result, people still enquire from time to time as to whether I want to find out what happened.

"Why don't you go back to the house and ask them?" they say.

Well, my answer is simple: No, thanks. I'd rather not know. In this case, ignorance is bliss; you can keep your bloody hours!

LOVE ADVENTURERS

The Wedding Jam
Paul Lescure, Stockport, UK

I PROPOSED TO KATHRYN AFTER five months. After only three weeks, I thought she'd be my wife if the truth be known. They say that relationships are all about compromise, and that's precisely why I'd struggled to find anyone who remotely fit the bill for 'potential wife'. Then I met Kathryn. She's the most exemplary person I've ever known, and we complement each other's lifestyles perfectly.

Sure, we have our own interests, but in key areas, they overlap. Take my computer, for instance; I adore it. Every woman I've ever been out with has had a big problem with this, but not Kathryn. She knows it makes me happy, and she wants me to be happy, so she actively encourages it. Another pastime is smoking, which has been a bone of contention in previous relationships, but not with Kathryn. I proposed to her while we were smoking in a coffee shop in Amsterdam. That's the kind of match we are.

We agreed from the outset that we didn't want a traditional wedding, as every ceremony we'd ever attended had been duller than a three-day finance convention. We were determined for ours to be the exact opposite.

One of our dreams was to walk down the aisle to the music of our choice, and definitely not the Wedding March. For years I thought the Wedding March sounded too similar to the Rocky theme music, Gonna Fly Now. You know the song that accompanies Rocky punching ten bells of shit out of a dead cow in a freezer. I'd vowed from an early age that should some poor schmuck ever want to marry me, it would not be to the Wedding March. On the most important day of my life, the last thing I wanted in my head was Sylvester Stallone punching a massive slab of meat.

Kathryn and I worshipped dance music when we met, so we quickly agreed on the genre. You may be surprised by our choice, but in comparison to my teenage fantasy, it was the better option by far. Back then, I thought there could be no more pleasing moment than walking down the aisle to Enter Sandman by Metallica. Although it's a damn fine tune, age has bought me wisdom, and I finally appreciate that it's not the most fitting song for a church.

So, dance music it was, but how do you pick one tune to accompany such a memorable thirty-metre walk? We set aside a few weekends and listened to every decent album we'd ever owned, making notes along the way. I became somewhat alarmed when reading back over the notes to see I'd given Super Sharp Shooter by Ganja Kru a respectable nine out of ten. Coming down the aisle to a dub tune about a sniper did not seem a bright idea in the cold light of day.

It took a few weekends, but eventually, we drew together a list of twelve of the finest tunes known to humanity. Picking one over the rest was now akin to choosing a best man or matron of honour, as eleven would miss out. Getting ruthless, we chopped the list down to a final three before coming to a standstill. To break the deadlock, I suggested that we play all three on a whim, to which Kathryn immediately agreed. We'd play one walking down the aisle, one signing the register, and the last as we walked out.

So, which would be the tune to replace the almighty Wedding March? Of our original shortlisted twelve, four were by Orbital, so we felt a strong connection that they should accompany us. And if it was going to be Orbital, there could only be one winner, Halcyon + On + On, the most beautiful tune in the world.

With that part decided, we turned our attention to finding a vicar who'd marry us to dance music in a church. The guy we found had unique morals and probably shouldn't have been a man of the cloth in the first place. He even scammed £20 out of my chief usher, Jas, waiting until all the guests had gone before telling him there was an outstanding balance on the wedding fees. Of course, not thinking that a vicar would try and con him, Jas paid up despite the fact I'd already squared the bill beforehand.

I began to have serious doubts about him during our wedding rehearsal. As we followed him down the aisle with Halcyon playing in the background, he started to dance with no rhythm or timing. It was as though we'd suddenly been transported to a contemporary dance gathering. Then, when we arrived at the altar, he turned around and said to us, "That Orbital track is quite funky, you know."

This caused me severe anxiety. If the vicar liked the tune we'd chosen, perhaps we had no idea what we were doing. Still, it was too late, and I'd have struggled to find a replacement who'd agree to such a unique wedding at twenty hours' notice. We decided that if we wanted to get married to dance music in a church, we'd do it on his watch.

The following afternoon, Kathryn and I got married on a day that couldn't have gone better. It was the sweetest day of my life. The only hiccup came just before our grand entrance when the first haunting bars of Halcyon wafted through the entrance doors, and I burst into tears. Thankfully I had a couple of minutes to compose myself before the bass kicked in, and we walked down the aisle together.

Funnily enough, despite all our planning, I don't remember much about the aisle walk, but I am grateful that the vicar didn't show off his awful dance moves the second time around.

Jas performed admirably with his DJ duties. Give It Away by Zero 7 accompanied the signing of the register while we perfectly timed our exit to All I Need by Air. After the ceremony, our friends told us that hearing Halcyon had given them goosebumps, which was precisely the reaction we'd hoped for.

Later that evening, rather than offering people sugared almonds during the reception, we provided CDs with the twelve shortlisted tracks we'd spent hours finding. Half an hour into the reception, all the CDs were gone, leaving a rather chuffed husband and wife in their place. We visit our guests nearly twenty years later and still see them enjoying the CD. It never gets dull hearing that people love listening to it; plus, who wants sugared bloody almonds when you can have a CD anyway?

Our unique wedding did have one major downside, though. Since that beautiful day, I've tried on many occasions to listen to Halcyon again, but every time it's like my body has an allergic reaction. I get heart palpitations with cold sweats and feel like Malcolm McDowell in A Clockwork Orange with someone playing Halcyon as an experiment on my brain. It sends me over the edge. Every. Single. Time.

I fear that the price I have to pay for walking down the aisle to the most incredible tune of all time is the inability ever to enjoy it again.

So, I ask myself, was it worth it?

You bet your sweet ass it was.

Love, And Then Lose

Robert Ahnston, San Franciso, US

LOVE, AND THEN LOSE. THIS may seem like something stupid to do, and I certainly don't say it with any intention that one should set out to lose at this or anything else in life for that matter. It's just another perspective on something that rarely seems to have any good effect.

After acquiring a few experiences in the world of relationships, most people will at some point have a story about 'the one that got away'. I'm no different. In fact, I'd say I've had two! Woe is me.

After graduating from college, I told myself that I was allowed to mess around for one year, maximum. From my perspective, I'd just completed 17 years of schooling and jumping straight into my career path seemed like a waste of a privilege of youth. I knew that at some point in my future, all of the irresponsible things I could get away with now were not as socially acceptable back then. For instance, coming home loudly drunk and puking in the front yard is something you can get away with when you're 21. When you're 41, it's not as well accepted, especially if you have kids.

Instead of getting a job that befit my degree, I looked for a job that could fund my social life without being too intrusive. As it went, I ended up at a flood zone research company. The job itself was pretty easy as I was probably overqualified for it, but what I liked most was the casual atmosphere that allowed me to socialise with my co-workers for most of the day. By my third month, I'd already gained enough knowledge of procedures to become a trainer of new staff. My first trainee was Katie.

When I first laid eyes on Katie, I was smitten. She had what a co-worker aptly described as a 'sombre elegance'. She wasn't a person who walked into a room and demanded attention like a movie star, and in a crowd of people, most would overlook her at first, but once you did spot her, she had radiance and charm that was difficult to erase from memory. In her preferred outfits of shorts and t-shirts, she could somehow hold your attention like a bride in her wedding dress. As she was my job trainee, I got to know her quickly and came to learn that her exterior beauty was only a fraction of her overall beauty.

I asked her to have a beer with me after the first week, and she agreed. Early in the evening's conversation, we started discussing what we'd do if we won the lotto. I said the usual clichéd ideas about travelling and acquiring particular material objects for myself. Still, I balanced this with putting some aside for those close to me and leaving the rest for charitable purposes. Katie, on the other hand, said she'd give all her winnings to charity. At the time, I didn't believe her. I thought she was talking herself up as a Mother Theresa type figure. At the very least, I thought she'd buy a house and then give the rest away. After we became close friends over the remainder of my year, she convinced me that she had never lied about that or about anything else she ever told me.

We learned that we lived near each other, and from that day on, we shared a ride to work. This was easily the single greatest factor that kept my attendance and promptness on a model employee basis. For the nine months we were at the flood zone company, I was always motivated to get there because I knew I'd be spending time with her. Away from our work, we went to movies, poetry recitals, caught the odd band, went to parties and generally hung out. To everyone around us, it would seem that we were two young lovers doing the things that two young lovers do. Only we weren't. Katie lived with another guy. Her boyfriend.

During the time I knew Katie, I dated other women and talked to her about them, and she discussed her relationship with me. In essence, we were friends, but we became closer than we were with anyone else in our lives during those nine months, spending much of our spare time together and opening our hearts entirely to one another. It didn't take long before there was a longing for the other in the background.

From my perspective, the thing that attracted me most was her purity of heart, and when I say this, I don't mean that she was a kind of Virgin Mary. Katie drank, sometimes smoked pot, laughed when I span my car out in parking lots, told dirty jokes and lived a life that would generally keep her out of a nunnery. Yet she was always caring and willing to give of herself. She'd spent time travelling through Africa and the Middle East, shaping her beliefs and learning about different cultures while she lived, studied, and participated in charity work. Katie was a brave person who'd give a ride to a homeless guy in the middle of the night despite the obvious dangers. It led me to believe that her giving nature defied her self-preservation instincts. I never heard her talking about fear, and I'm inclined to believe that she didn't have any.

My time with Katie culminated in her car one night after a long day of visiting friends around town. She was about to quit the research job, and I wasn't far behind her as my year was coming to an end. I knew I was in love with her by then, but I never truly acted on it. She'd leave her boyfriend for me in an ideal world, but I, perhaps cowardly, never wanted to force the issue. In a way, I thought that if she did leave her boyfriend, it would somehow destroy this angelic image I had of her. Was she as unselfish as I believed her to be if she broke his heart? That night, after sharing our feelings about each other, I moved to get out of her car, and she pulled me back in by my hand. I remember staring into those eyes and seeing what I thought were tears welling up and a longing for the impossible. We kissed each other very slowly and then sat in silence for a long while afterwards.

I spent the summer out of the country, and Katie moved to Massachusetts with her boyfriend. After returning, I moved away from Austin to San Diego. I called her once, and we spoke for a while, but we never spoke again after that. At the time, I had many other things going on in my life, and she only seemed to be a sad reminder of unrequited love. To this day, I don't feel a need to call her. I've accepted that the moment has passed, and there is nothing left to do. I imagine that she either married her boyfriend or went back to Africa to do some voluntary work that would give focus to her giving heart.

It has been many years now. Whenever I think of her, there's a small amount of desire that I wish it would have worked out differently, but mostly I'm happy in the knowledge that it worked out the best it could under the circumstances. In the short time we knew each other, she convinced me she was an angel, and there is nothing in my memory to make me doubt it. I wrote her a poem once, trying to explain what I thought was our situation. I gave it to her before we parted, and I hope she still has it.

For us, I feel it's left to another lifetime and another world, but I'm grateful to have experienced a piece of it in this one.

My First Love
Maeve Donnellan, Moycullen, Ireland

IN 1945 MY PARENTS BOUGHT their first house near Galway in the west of Ireland. Until then, my three sisters and I lived in chaotic harmony with my grandmother, six miles away. My hardworking parents were schoolteachers and cycled considerable distances to and from work each day, saving for the time when they'd buy their first house.

Eventually, they did, and our clan moved into 'Dovepark' on a glorious August summer's day. I remember running through the orchards in the first few days, smelling the Beauty of Bath apples, red and rosy. In the fields beyond, my sisters and I climbed trees, rolled down grassy slopes and bathed our dolls in the holes of the limestone rocks. We had such freedom. My mother blew a loud whistle when meals were ready, and we raced home to the waft of her homemade bread and scones filling the air as we burst into the kitchen with wholesome pangs of hunger.

After school, each family member had their chore. My mother prepared the evening meal while my sisters tidied the bedrooms, and my father brought in wood and coal for the fires and vegetables from the garden. My job was to care for two-dozen Rhode Island Red hens.

"*Chuck, chuck, chuck,*" I called to them as they came running to be fed. I counted their still-warm eggs into my basket, careful not to crack or damage this valuable addition to our larder. I cleaned their nesting boxes and filled them with fresh straw, making them comfortable for the night. Then, before darkness descended, they were called, counted, and safely secured from Mr Fox, cackling furiously with indignation for ending their day too soon. In all the years, there was never a hen lost on my watch. The rest of the evening was spent on homework, as there was no television.

One day my father announced that he had a surprise for us, another sister we assumed as their original four girls had now become seven, so we gathered around to hear the news. She arrived exquisitely beautiful, big, majestic, serene, and with the most expressive brown eyes you have ever seen. She spoke, "*Moooooooo*," and I was smitten; it was love at first sight. She was our very own cow, and we called her Alice.

As time went by, I acquired a second chore, and once my hens had been seen to, I now also cleaned Alice's byre, which adjoined the henhouse. I gathered armfuls of fresh ferns from the fields outside and left them strewn over the floor where she slept. Then I would leave her manger full of fresh hay. When her byre was ready, I'd wander up through the fields calling, "*A-lice, A-lice,*" and she'd come to me mooing softly. Next up, I had the adventure of learning how to milk her.

After walking back together, I'd get to work. She didn't need tethering as I retrieved my stool and white bucket, set them down and filled the pail with her warm frothy milk. Milking a cow is an art form, and like cycling, once you get the hang of it, you never forget how it's done. As I sat there milking her, she chewed satisfyingly on the hay, mooing softly with what I took to be gratitude. "*Nice, Alice,*" I whispered. "*Nice, Alice.*"

Summers then were long balmy days with seemingly endless blue skies. While my older sisters cooked and sewed, making clothes to wear to Seapoint Ballroom, I could be found in a nearby field with Alice. She would lie chewing the cud amongst the daisies and clover while I lay into her soft, warm belly with a book. 'What Katy Did' and 'What Katy Did Next' were two I remember reading as Alice mooed contently. Occasionally she'd get up to wander into the woods, but she always returned to take her old position. Alice and me. Me and Alice.

But it wasn't all blue skies and What Katy Did or Did Next, oh no. If summers seemed warmer, winters were longer and colder. I groaned as I left my bed at 7 am to see to my chores. The windows were frosted on the inside, and we had no central heating or thickly padded jackets to warm us. After a quick wash and even quicker dress, I walked to the cowshed with my bucket. On the way, I opened the hen house door to release and feed them, despite their reluctance to leave the safe, warm haven.

After filling Alice's manger with hay, I'd sit to milk her, almost lulling myself back to broken, unfinished dreams with the long 'swish, swish, swish' of warm milk hitting the frothy pail. Gradually the strokes grew weaker and weaker until I knew her udder was empty. I almost envied her as I shut her in for the day; too cold to wander the fields. I strained her warm milk through muslin into jugs, where it sat cooling on large slabs of white marble in the pantry - we didn't have a fridge either. My sisters and I gobbled down porridge with brown bread and tea before my father shouted, "Leaving in five minutes," and so began the school day.

Years passed, and secondary education loomed in the distance like a giant precipice. I was 12, and Alice was much older in cow years now, not producing the same amount of milk as she once did. I returned from boarding school in December 1953 to find she was gone. As I cried my bitter tears, nobody told me why she'd gone or where she'd gone to, and I was too afraid to ask for fear of what the answer might be.

Polly was now in Alice's byre, walking Alice's fields, eating Alice's clover. We never connected, Polly and me. She was just a cow with no character. My Alice was irreplaceable.

Backpack or Bucket List

Aarti Amin, UK

I'VE NEVER BEEN THE TYPE of woman to coo over a baby or bond instantly with every child that crosses my path. In fact, without thinking, I must have upset a fair number of people over the years with my lack of affection for their offspring.

As those around me met their partners, spawned mini-me's, and settled into family living, I was busy backpacking the world, experiencing different cultures and meeting people from all walks of life. Even after I settled into my first 'grown up' job, I mostly spent my time planning the next adventure for me and my backpack.

Hence, I distinctly remember a turning point when maybe, just maybe, I hoped for something more from life. Bucket lists were becoming increasingly popular, and in 2003 the BBC produced a list of '50 things to experience before you die'. My competitive edge kicked in, so I started going through the list to prove what a seasoned backpacker I was and hopefully gloat in my new status of super traveller and adventurer extraordinaire.

- Go white water rafting – tick
- Dive the Great Barrier Reef – tick
- Visit the Grand Canyon – tick
- Hike the Inca Trail – tick
- And coming in as the undoubted winner at number one? Swim with dolphins - TICK AND TICK (and in the wild too)

Maybe I can put it down to the glasses of wine or the battle I was having about whether my backpack and I should stay in the UK or take off travelling again, but as I reread the list, I questioned that whilst the experiences were incredible, were they life-changing? And should I die tomorrow, would my final thoughts be how grateful I was that I'd been able to swim with dolphins?

At that exact moment, I realised that becoming someone's mum was at the top of my bucket list. I knew that I was in no rush to become a mother and that I'd want it to happen under the right circumstances, with the right person, and at the right time. In fact, over the years, I came to accept that it might not happen at all.

The following 12 years brought more unforgettable travels, overseas jobs, successful dates, unsuccessful dates, a proper grown-up job, a house, and ultimately meeting the man who has helped me tick off my number one thing to experience before I die.

When we found out we were expecting our first baby, we were thrilled and daunted in equal measure. Our lives as we'd once known them were about to sail into the sunset, and we could now identify with concerns we'd previously only ever heard about. Would we be good parents? Would our relationship survive? Was it ok that we felt completely clueless?

We signed up for local childbirth classes where we learned in gruesome detail how my body would change over the coming months. I'd always stated that you shouldn't squeeze a watermelon out of a hole that small, but it was about to be! I'm a self-proclaimed wuss and found the thought of giving birth quite daunting, so I even dragged my poor husband along to a full day of hypnobirth training to try and deal with my anxiety.

As a vet, I've witnessed cats and dogs pushing out their offspring as easily as they would (a very firm) pooh and then seen their little ones begin to suckle immediately. So it was with slightly amused resignation I realised how inept humans are at reproducing. It takes us nearly ten months to produce a single, viable baby that then has to learn to feed. I didn't even know that breastfeeding didn't 'just happen' until I had a baby. We could certainly learn a thing or two from cats and dogs!

As the start of my maternity leave approached, my expanding belly became a barrier to being able to work effectively. My tolerance and temper shortened, and with a sigh of relief, I worked my last day and prepared for four weeks of relaxation. I should have known that no child of mine would be late, and our baby girl arrived three weeks earlier than expected! I rushed to the hospital, and after several discussions and tears (my 15-year-old cat was also being put to sleep that day), a caesarian section was agreed. My inner wuss heaved a massive sigh of relief... thank god I wouldn't have to push a watermelon out of that hole!

Now you know the background, I'd like to focus on the feeling of being someone's mum. I understand that this is not something everyone desires and having experienced three miscarriages, my heart goes out to those unable to fulfil their dreams of becoming a mother or father.

At the time of writing, our little girl is 15 months old and has recently started walking and talking and making us laugh out loud daily. We've reached a stage where she is a delight every single day, and our hearts are overflowing with how blessed we feel to have her in our lives.

I am, however, under no illusion that growing a little person is easy. Having a baby is a multifaceted job and one that everyone has their opinion on. You have all types of parenting, from the followers of the disciplined, strict routine to the earth mothers who believe that the babies should dictate what you do. In the emotional, tired, fragile state that follows childbirth, this can be daunting and leave you feeling like the worst of mothers. Ironically, even though you are with another person 24 hours a day, it can also be the most lonely of times as you struggle to meet new people through a foggy mind of sleep deprivation and change management.

Luckily, my mother is a health professional who has worked with children for over 45 years. Her advice was simple: "She's a baby, and she needs you, so look after her and give her what she wants, but make sure you look after yourself. If the parents are ok, the child will be ok". There's a reason why mothers are known for their wise words of wisdom.

The number of memories I have would bore you to tears. However, the parenthood adventure is the most incredible and profound emotion I've ever felt, combined with the most frustrating and self-doubting. For instance, with parenthood comes responsibility. One day I took my car to be valeted, and after checking I had my phone, keys and wallet, I began to walk away. Moments later, I heard a shout calling me back as I'd left a baby in the car!

Then there's the quantity of vomit and pooh – it's real. Poohnamis do exist, and generally at the most inconvenient of moments. On more than one occasion, my baby, bedclothes, and own pyjamas all had to be stripped and washed immediately after a tidal wave of bodily fluids struck during the middle of the night!

Also, I worry constantly. I worried before, but not like this. Previously it was things like whether people liked me, had I upset someone, and was I good enough? Now magnify those feelings by 1000, and that's how motherhood can feel.

I worry about the world I've brought my girl into. I worry whether she'll be persecuted in the future because of her heritage. I worry that one day I can't be there to protect her. I worry that I'll make irreversible mistakes as a parent. I worry that she'll move overseas, far away from me. And I worry that she might not even like her mum one day, never mind love her.

However, this is entirely natural, and I'm sure it is how most parents feel. It's the reality of parenthood.

But would I change any of it for a second? Hell, no! Hearing my girl shouting "Mammy" at me and poking my face as she delights in that she's found my 'nose' is just the best feeling. Her morning hugs make my day, and my family makes having a baby a pleasure as they help look after her around my work commitments and desire to travel.

In the interim between writing this story and publishing it, it would be fair to say we've been busy. Amongst a job change, house move, and a global pandemic, we've welcomed our gorgeous son into the world. Bringing a second child into the mix has added to the challenge of parenthood, taking sleep deprivation and brain fog to a whole new level. Despite the challenges, my opinion is that going from no children to 1 was far more demanding and compromising than going from 1 to 2. Life, as I'd known it for so many years, had already changed, so the adjustment this time was less daunting, and I'd like to think I wasn't quite so clueless.

Our boy has grown into a cheeky, happy little soul who gives the best of cuddles unexpectedly and unconditionally. The children adore each other (mostly) and enjoy spending time in each other's company. I've now reached the point where I want grandfather time to slow down and let me have my kids at this gorgeous young age for a while longer. I've heard it said that when you have children, 'the days are long but the years are short', and I can now start to grasp what this means. So a little note to my beautiful babies - don't grow so fast!

I feel supremely privileged that I've been able to fulfil my personal 'Number one thing to experience before I die'. Unsurprisingly, it's also helped me gain a deeper appreciation of how lucky I've been to travel extensively before parenthood.

As for me and my backpack, well, for a while, at least, the backpack is on an extended sabbatical. However, one day I am sure we will start our journey again, but this time with a husband and children in tow to add to those unforgettable memories that go hand in hand with travelling.

There's life in the old bucket list yet.

THE END

AFTERWORD

WHOA, IT'S OVER! YOU'VE MADE it through a rollercoaster of stories and experiences, so give yourself a well-deserved pat on the back. You've travelled around the world, from the Northern Lights in Scandinavia to beautiful vineyards in the Loire Valley, from the heights of the Himalayas to starry nights in the Caribbean. Heck, I'm going to pat myself on the back for presenting all of these stories, not to mention living through getting them. I hope you've enjoyed reading them as much as I've enjoyed putting them together.

Life wouldn't have been so kind to me without the combined luck of a whole leprechaun convention and taking my chances when they presented themselves. Undeniably, my supportive network of family and friends has helped me out of my comfort zone to embrace new cultures, experiences, and people. If it hadn't been for them, I'd never have been able to collect all these fantastic tales.

You get one chance at the game of life, and while you're young, you'll have more opportunity and freedom than it's possible to appreciate. As the years pass, your responsibility to others may increase, and openings for exploration and adventure may lessen. Bones will age, partners and small people may appear (wrinkles too), aches and pains will set in, and recovery from exertion begins to take two days instead of one!

Don't let these years creep by without gaining some valuable life experience of what it's like to feel alive. Really alive. Search for experiences that will help you understand how to inhale and exhale life. Wake up every day and learn to feel young in your mind, body and heart because there will come a day when you won't feel invincible anymore. Remember to take your precautions and know your limits, for your health and safety are paramount to your happiness and personal development.

Now you've read through these experiences, I hope they give you the energy and enthusiasm to have new ones. Don't forget to keep your ideas and ambitions close by, as this will help you stay focused and make sure that when your eyes are diverted from the bigger picture, it isn't permanent.

Good luck on your adventures, whatever they might be!

ACKNOWLEDGEMENTS

I RECEIVED A TREMENDOUS AMOUNT of support and encouragement during the research, writing and editing of this book. For my immediate family, I am indebted to you for helping to mould my views and experiences of the world, a moulding that made this book a realisation.

My incredible wife Aarti and two adorable children, Tanya and Liam, thank you for being the centre of my world, my yin and yang, my strength when I'm weak and my music in my soul. Your support is unwavering and I know you'd go to the ends of the earth with me.

My Mum and Dad looking down on me, brothers Brendan, Conor and Brian, sisters-in-law Julie and Lisa, nephew Luke and nieces Sarah, Anna and Ruby, thank you all for making me a proud son, brother and uncle. Thank you to my stepfather Mike, also a star in the sky, and his children Andrew, Martin and Jacqui, for being a rock to us when we lost our Dad. You treated my Mum like a queen and she laughed like a teenager with you. To my extended Donnellan and Hogan families that stretch to the four corners of the world, you are always in my heart. To my family in law, Vijay, Manda, Jag and Mayu, thanks for always being there. We appreciate your support immensely.

My generous, dedicated and adventurous writers, thanks a million to you all. Had it not been for your contributions and commitment, this book wouldn't exist. I was incredibly lucky to have so many people write their stories for this book and I know many stories didn't quite make it, but your offerings were truly appreciated and will always sit in my heart. To those who proof read, offered words of support when I'd given up, and those who still talk me into adventures, I am truly blessed to have you in my lives. Thank you, thank you, thank you.

Big shout outs to Aarti Amin, Bobby Ahn, Paras Purohit, Raj Sharma, Neil Mandt and Peter Burns. Without you this book would have probably taken another 20 years! Your kind, inspired words, generous help, and accompaniment in general life adventure will remain with me for the rest of my days. Proper legends.

Printed in Great Britain
by Amazon